LONGMAN IMPRINT BOOKS

Genres

A collection of styles and forms

Selected and edited by Geoff Barton

General editor: Michael Marland
Series consultant: Geoff Barton

Longman Imprint Books

General Editor: Michael Marland

New Titles

Global Tales
Introducing Media
Mystery & Horror
Starting Shakespeare
Stories Old and New
War Stories

Previously published titles

A Roald Dahl Selection
Autobiographies
Characters from Pre-20th Century Novels
Cider with Rosie Laurie Lee
Diaries and Letters
Diary of Anne Frank edited by Christopher Martin
Genres
Ghost Stories selected by Susan Hill
Highlights from 19th-Century Novels
I'm the King of the Castle Susan Hill
Landmarks
P'tang, Yang, Kipperbang and other TV plays Jack Rosenthal
Scenes from Plays
Stories from Africa
Stories from Asia
Ten Short Plays
The Human Element and other stories Stan Barstow
The Woman in Black Susan Hill
Travel Writing
Two Centuries

Contents

Non-Fiction

Introduction

Imagine it's the year 2006. You're sitting at your home computer and tapping the keyboard. Some text comes up on screen from somewhere on the Internet:

> The strong and the weak. May remembered those words when a movement downstairs woke her in the night...

You haven't read this before and you don't know what it is. But from the billions of words that have ever been written, you can begin to work out what type of text this might be. Fact or fiction? The word 'May' hints at a character: we seem to be looking inside her mind at what she remembered. She hears a noise and so do we. We quickly narrow this down to fiction: it has some features of story-telling. But what type of story is it? Science fiction, a ghost story, crime fiction...?

Based on the extract on your screen it's difficult to tell, but notice the way we can use our expectations to narrow down the possibilities. A text that started, 'He also wrote a number of film scripts, including *You Only Live Twice* (1967) and *Chitty Chitty Bang Bang*,' sends out different signals. It has the features of a non-fiction text and we certainly wouldn't begin to think that we had found our way into a collection of short stories.

This is what a genre is – a category of writing. When we begin a text, we already know certain basic things about it – for example, whether it is in a book, in a magazine or newspaper, or on a computer screen. We usually have certain expectations about a text before we read it: we expect a newspaper or magazine to contain short pieces of text aimed at informing or entertaining us. We assume that a novel will take longer to read, will contain made-up characters who form part of a story-line. In other words, we usually expect fiction (made-up stories) to feel different from non-fiction or factual texts. We want a recipe book to give precise information in an easy-to-read way: to come across characters and a story-line in this genre would be most unexpected and probably irritating.

This book gives you a chance to explore the way writers work within a variety of genres. Within fiction, you can look at the key features of science fiction or crime writing or horror. What do you expect when you read a horror story? It certainly won't be the same set of expectations as reading a computer instruction manual. Similarly, we know that non-fiction genres differ. We know that a speech will be different from a diary entry – but how will it differ?

Genres draws together a variety of types of writing, so that you can examine their different styles and your differing expectations when you approach them. Of course it would be foolish and misleading to suggest that any of the extracts in this book are 'typical' of their genre: a representative sci-fi story or autobiography would be difficult to find. If they existed, they would be dry formulas rather than lively texts that we would want to read. That is why two texts are usually included within each genre – to hint at the wide variety of texts that might be classified in this way.

I hope you find the choices of texts illuminating and thought-provoking. But most of all, I hope you enjoy reading them.

Geoff Barton

Ghost stories

The writer L. P. Hartley said that the ghost story was the most difficult form of fiction to write successfully: 'There is almost no intermediate step between success and failure. Either it comes off or it is a flop.' What are the key ingredients? Believable places and characters, tension, a precise written style, something supernatural, and – of course – fear . . .

Not at Home

by Jean Richardson

There were no lights in the bike shed and the bushes round about, which in daylight were an insignificant school-uniform green, loomed menacingly and cast fingers of shadow over the path.

Fetching her bike was the thing Alison hated most about staying late at school, though she usually had Joanne's cheerful company and the two of them together were brave enough to enjoy a few shivers. But Joanne had a sore throat, and although she had insisted on coming to school because it was English and she wanted her essay back, she had no voice for choir practice.

'But it was worth it,' she told Alison, her face flushed with pleasure and a temperature. '"A minus and a nice feeling for words."'

It would have been showing off in anyone else, but Alison knew how much being good at English mattered to Joanne. It made up for not being good at sport and a coward at vaulting and climbing a rope.

'You'd be up it fast enough if there was a fire,' Miss Barry had said unsympathetically, and several girls who were jealous of Joanne had tittered.

But Joanne didn't care. She felt she was the wrong shape to climb a rope and saw herself, in an emergency, being saved by a handsome fireman. She was always making up stories. It was she who referred to the old bike at the far end of the shed as a skeleton and suggested that the school caretaker lurked there after dark, hoping to catch a nice plump little girl for his supper.

It was nonsense, of course. Old Trayner didn't look very attractive, with decayed teeth that you couldn't help noticing when he smiled, but he was probably lonely and only wanted someone to talk to.

Nevertheless Alison was in a greater hurry than usual to find the key to her padlock. She had been late that morning and the only space had been at the far end, next to the 'skeleton'. No one knew whose bike it was nor why it had been abandoned, but the mudguards and chain had gone and the rust and cobwebs had moved in. Cobwebs . . . Spiders . . .

Alison jerked her bike free. In her hurry she had forgotten to remove her front lamp, and someone had nicked it. Blast! It was fatal to leave a lamp or a pump behind. Trayner probably had a thriving business in lamps and pumps, though most people suspected Finn's gang, who all had sticky fingers. Oh well, perhaps Dad would get her a dynamo at last.

She fumbled in her satchel for her safety belt. Books, ruler, Biros, and something that felt like crumbs or sand. No, it wasn't there. Then she remembered that it had wrapped itself round a book and she had put it in her desk. The door was probably still unlocked, but she didn't fancy crossing the dark hall and going upstairs and along the corridor to 2B. Schools were designed to be full of people; empty they were scary places, unnaturally quiet, as though everyone was dead. She'd have to do without her belt. It surely wouldn't matter just for once, though she had promised to wear it every day. It was something her mother had insisted on when she agreed to let Alison cycle to school.

She wedged her satchel in her basket and patted her saddle. Although she wouldn't have admitted it to

Joanne, Alison thought of her bike as a trusty steed, and it was comforting to feel that she had an ally who would help her make a quick getaway.

She decided to risk cycling down the drive. They were not supposed to, but there were no lights in the head's study and she doubted whether Miss Cliffe, who lived opposite the school and was fond of keeping an eye on things even when off-duty, would be glued to her window on a winter evening. More likely she'd be toasting her sturdy legs in front of the fire.

It seemed much darker without a front lamp, though its light was only small and wavering. The damp air tangled Alison's hair into frizzy curls and she shivered. They didn't have real fogs nowadays, not the kind you read about in Dickens, where people had to grope their way through the streets, but there were rags of mist and the street lamps had garish yellow haloes.

Alison sang to herself as she cycled along.

'The holly bears a berry as red as any blood,
And Mary bore sweet Jesus Christ for to do poor sinners good.'

They had been practising for the end-of-term concert, and her head rang with glorias and tidings of comfort and joy. It was less than a month to Christmas, and the very thought warmed her.

She reached a crossroads and now had to turn right into the main road. It was always a moment she dreaded, because the traffic raced along and she hadn't the nerve to take a quick chance.

She looked to the right, to the left, and then to the right again and stuck her arm out, though it seemed daft to signal when she wasn't very visible. She was halfway across when a car shot out impatiently from the other side of the crossroads. Startled, Alison swerved and then wobbled as her shoe slipped off the pedal and grazed the road, and at that moment a container lorry as tall as a house and as long as a train came hurtling towards her. It was going fast, and the swish of its hot breath seemed to suck her in towards the giant tyres. It happened so quickly: she felt as though she were being drawn into a black void while two red eyes, which she realised afterwards must have been the brake lights of the car, blazed fiercely before being extinguished by the mist.

And then Alison found herself alone in the road. She was trembling, and she felt off-balance and as though her body didn't quite belong to her. Her heart was still pounding as she began to push her bike along, but it was too far to walk all the way. 'It's like falling off a horse,' she told herself. 'I must get on again or I shall lose my nerve.'

If only Mum would be there when she got home, but her mother worked part-time and had a late meeting. Peter might be home, but he wasn't prepared to say what he was up to these days, at least not to a sister. Alison enjoyed getting her own tea, but having the house all to herself was a bit creepy, especially at first, when it was so still she thought someone was there and holding his breath.

She turned into the Avenue, and took the third turning on the right and then down Fernhead. The houses were semi-detached, with bay windows and stubby front gardens behind privet hedges. Mum had promised to leave the light on, but she must have forgotten for the house was in darkness.

Alison pushed open the gate with her bike. The hedge seemed taller than usual and showered her with rain-drops. It really was time Dad cut it, though he always said as an excuse that hedges didn't grow in winter. She scrabbled in her pocket for the key. Soggy tissues ... purse ... the button off her raincoat ... here it was. She felt for the lock and opened the door. The light switch was halfway along the wall, which meant that she had to plunge into blackness.

In her haste she banged her knee on something hard with a sharp corner. It took her by surprise and her heart thumped as she felt for the switch and pressed it down.

She had banged her knee on a large carved wooden chest that she had never seen before. She sensed at once that the hall was different. The carpet was the same. And there was that mark on it where Peter had upset a tin of paint. The walls were the same colour, but the two watercolours her gran had done on holiday were missing and in their place was a poster advertising a railway museum.

Alison looked round in bewilderment. She was in two minds about shutting the front door, because it seemed more frightening inside than out. Was she seeing things? Was she in the right house? She looked down at the telephone standing on the mysterious wooden chest and checked. Yes, it was the right number. Of course it was. Her mother was fond of saying they needed a change, and swapping round the pictures was just the sort of thing she liked doing. And it was just like her to forget to tell them that she'd bought a chest, because her father would then point out that they didn't need a chest because they'd got enough old junk of their own already. Yes, that must be what had happened.

She shut the front door and went upstairs to her room.

Only it wasn't her room any more. It belonged to someone who could have been about her age, but this person had a scarlet chest of drawers and wardrobe with a desk unit slotted between them. They were so much what Alison herself would have liked, that for a moment she wondered whether her parents had got rid of the old wardrobe that had belonged to Gran and the rickety table she used as a desk, and bought these smart units as a giant Christmas present.

But what had they done with her things? The clothes spilling out of the wardrobe weren't hers. She didn't wear long skirts or that vivid shade of pink. And what had Mum done with her books and the old toys that she couldn't bear to throw away ...?

She went along the landing into Peter's room. It was even untidier than usual: there were stacks of computer magazines and a workbench strewn with little tins of paint and brushes and glue and a half-finished model aeroplane. That was something Peter would never have the patience to make.

Alison was standing in the doorway of her parents' transformed bedroom when she heard the front door open.

It must be Peter, and she was about to call out and run downstairs to him when something stopped her. Everything was so different, so unexpected, that perhaps Peter might be changed in some dreadful way too.

She tiptoed across to the stairs, aware that she didn't want to be seen. She heard voices, and then someone slammed the front door.

'Danny! You've let the cat out.' It was a woman's voice.

'It wasn't my fault. He ran out before I could stop him.' The boy sounded younger than Peter.

'Well, don't blame me if he gets run over. You know how dangerous that road is. The Walkers' cat was killed last week and the traffic shoots along now it's one-way.'

'It doesn't make any difference if you let him out at

the back. He's learned how to get round.' This was a girl, who went into the front room and switched on the television while the boy and the woman disappeared into the kitchen. Alison heard a tap running and then the sound of a kettle being plugged in.

She felt an intruder. They sounded like a normal family coming back to their own home, and what would they do when they found a stranger there? Would they believe that it had been her home that morning, that she and her brother and her parents had lived there for the past seven years? More likely they'd think she'd broken in and send for the police. And would *they* believe her? Alison saw herself trying to convince a disbelieving unsympathetic inspector that she had left the house that very morning and that the key that opened the front door was hers ...

No, she must get out of the house as quickly as possible.

'It's upstairs. I'll go and get it.' The boy appeared in the hall and Alison ducked back into her bedroom. She held her breath as she heard him run up the stairs. Please let whatever he wanted be in his own room!

The door was just open, and she saw the boy go past with a jersey. There was a smell of frying, and Alison thought longingly of her own tea. She had been planning to have fish fingers and baked beans with oven-ready chips.

'In here or in there?' called the woman.

'In here. I want to watch tele.'

'Well, come and get it.'

There was a clatter of knives and forks and people went to and from the kitchen. Alison moved to the top of the stairs. The front-room door was shut and they all seemed to be in there having their tea. Please don't let them have forgotten the salt or the ketchup!

She slid down the stairs, ran to the front door and out into the night. Something jumped on her and she half-screamed before she realised that it was the cat. It was as startled as she was, and fled under the hedge.

At least her bike was still there, invisible in the shadows. She grabbed it and stumbled out into the street. There seemed to be more traffic than usual, coming towards her on both sides of the road, and she remembered the woman saying that it was a one-way street. But it hadn't been. Not that morning.

I must have made a mistake, she told herself. It's the wrong street but somehow my key fitted their front door. Was it possible? But the phone number was the right one and the sign at the end of the street, when she reached it, said unmistakably 'Fernhead Road'.

Alison was near to tears. She was cold and frightened and alone, and she longed for her mother and the safety and security of her own home. Even Peter would have been welcome. He must be due home whatever he'd been up to, and he would find everything changed as she had done.

She cycled past the little public garden that always shut early in winter. That at least looked the same. She was now approaching the high street where there was a straggling parade of shops. There was Aziz where they bought sweets and newspapers, the Chinese takeaway, a fish and chip shop and a pub called The Frog and Nightdress. There couldn't be another pub with a name like that! Home must be somewhere nearby. Perhaps if she were to go back to Fernhead Road she would find that it had all been some ghastly mistake or a bad dream.

And then Alison saw that something had changed. On Saturday she had noticed a new hoarding that had gone up on some waste ground at one end of the shops. It said that the site had been acquired by a chain of supermarkets and now, only four days later, there was the new supermarket.

Wonderingly she wheeled her bike towards it. There was even a rack of cycles outside, and as though in a dream she parked hers and went in.

It was the largest supermarket she had ever seen. Avenues of shelves stretched away into the distance and frozen cabinets half a mile long were stacked with regiments of turkeys, ducks and geese. Boxes of mince pies and Christmas puddings were stacked in a pyramid crowned by a plastic Christmas tree with winking lights, and a carol, arranged for some vast invisible orchestra, wafted through the air as though on the wings of an aerosol.

Most of the customers wheeled trolleys piled so high that they might have been shopping for expeditions to the North Pole or the Andes, while boys in holly-green aprons replenished the shelves or hurried up and down the aisles checking queries relayed to them by two-way radio. Some of them didn't look much older than Alison, and she tried to pluck up the courage to speak to a boy who was shovelling brazils into a counter of nuts. There was something familiar about him, she realised. He reminded her of Sean Maloney, who was in her class, but it couldn't be him because they weren't allowed to take jobs, even part-time. She knew there were lots of Maloneys, so he must be an older brother with the same tight coppery curls.

But what could she say? He'd think she was a nutter if she asked him how they could possibly have built, stocked and staffed a supermarket in four days!

She had just decided to ask him, as an opener, where the milk was, when she saw a familiar face further down the aisle. It was Joanne's mother, Mrs Cullen, and she was reaching for some mince pies.

It was better than the best Christmas present. Everything was going to be all right, even if it was rather puzzling. She would tell Mrs Cullen about the house and perhaps go back and have tea with Joanne while it was all sorted out.

She ran down the aisle. Mrs Cullen had her back to Alison so didn't see her coming.

'Mrs Cullen, am I glad to see you. I don't know what's happened –'

Alison got no further, because when Joanne's mother saw her, she made a funny little choking noise and crumpled up as though Alison had shot her. She fell against the display and mince pies and Christmas puddings skated along the aisles while the tree lurched forward, its lights flashing a wild signal of distress.

'She's having a fit,' said one woman. 'I think she's fainted,' said another, but neither of them made any move to help. A girl from the checkout, who had done a course in first aid, propped up Mrs Cullen and asked for a glass of water.

Mrs Cullen opened her eyes. She seemed dazed.

'I think she's only fainted,' said the checkout girl. 'Can someone get a chair?'

Sean Maloney, looking a mixture of embarrassed and inquisitive, brought one.

Mrs Cullen recognised him. 'Did you see her?' she asked faintly.

'See who?'

'That girl. The one who came up to me. She ... she ...' Mrs Cullen was crying.

'I didn't see any girl.' Several customers were looking at Sean as though he were somehow to blame.

'It wasn't *any* girl. You must remember her. She was in your class. She was Joanne's friend. Alison Potter.'

'Alison Potter!' Sean Maloney backed away. 'But it

couldn't have been her. She was ...' He didn't like to say it.

'Killed,' said Mrs Cullen with a shudder. 'That's right. She was run over and killed on the way home from school. The Potters lived in our road, but they moved after the accident.'

'You must have imagined it,' said Sean. 'Or seen someone who looked like her.'

He looked round at the shoppers, most of whom had moved away now that there was nothing to see but a frightened-looking woman on a chair. He remembered Alison Potter, but there was no sign of her, or of any girl who looked remotely like her.

I Used to Live Here Once

by Jean Rhys

She was standing by the river looking at the stepping-stones and remembering each one. There was the round unsteady stone, the pointed one, the flat one in the middle – the safe stone where you could stand and look round. The next wasn't so safe, for when the river was full the water flowed over it and even when it showed dry it was slippery. But after that it was easy and soon she was standing on the other side.

The road was much wider than it used to be but the work had been done carelessly. The felled trees had not been cleared away and the bushes looked trampled. Yet it was the same road and she walked along feeling extraordinarily happy.

It was a fine day, a blue day. The only thing was that the sky had a glassy look that she didn't remember. That was the only word she could think of. Glassy. She turned the corner, saw that what had been the old pavé had been taken up, and there too the road was much wider, but it had the same unfinished look.

She came to the worn stone steps that led up to the house and her heart began to beat. The screw pine was gone, so was the mock summer-house called the ajoupa, but the clove tree was still there and at the top of the steps the rough lawn stretched away, just as she remembered it. She stopped and looked towards the house that had been added to and painted white. It was strange to see a car standing in front of it.

There were two children under the big mango tree, a boy and a little girl, and she waved to them and called 'Hallo' but they didn't answer her or turn their heads. Very fair children, as Europeans born in the West Indies so often are: as if the white blood is asserting itself against all odds.

The grass was yellow in the hot sunlight as she walked towards them. When she was quite close she called again, shyly: 'Hallo.' Then, 'I used to live here once,' she said.

Still they didn't answer. When she said for the third time 'Hallo' she was quite near them. Her arms went out instinctively with the longing to touch them.

It was the boy who turned. His grey eyes looked straight into hers. His expression didn't change. He said: 'Hasn't it gone cold all of a sudden. D'you notice? Let's go in.' 'Yes let's,' said the girl.

Her arms fell to her sides as she watched them running across the grass to the house. That was the first time she knew.

Crime fiction

What makes for good crime writing? Writer Mary Roberts Rinehart said that a mystery story was really two stories in one: 'the story of what happened and the story of what appeared to happen'. The key ingredients: a crime (of course!), some element of mystery (whodunit or why?), a precise, realistic style, and – usually – an investigator whose eyes we see through ...

May and June

by Ruth Rendell

Their parents named them May and June because their birthdays occurred in those months. A third sister, an April child, had been christened Avril but she had died. May was like the time of year in which she had been born, changeable, chilly and warm by turns, sullen yet able to know and show a loveliness that couldn't last.

In the nineteen thirties, when May was in her twenties, it was still important to get one's daughters well married, and though Mrs Thrace had no anxieties on that head for sunny June, she was less sanguine with regard to May. Her elder daughter was neither pretty nor graceful nor clever, and no man had ever looked at her twice. June, of course, had a string of admirers. Then May met a young lawyer at a *thé dansant*. His name was Walter Symonds, he was extremely good looking, his father was wealthy and made him a generous allowance, and there was no doubt he belonged in a higher social class than that of the Thraces. May fell passionately in love with him, but no one was more surprised than she when he asked her to marry him.

The intensity of her passion frightened Mrs Thrace. It wasn't quite nice. The expression on her face while she awaited the coming of her fiancé, her ardour when she greeted him, the hunger in her eyes – that sort of thing was all very well in the cinema, but unsuitable for a civil servant's daughter in a genteel suburb.

Briefly, she had become almost beautiful. 'I'm going

to marry him,' she said when warned. 'He wants me to love him, doesn't he? He loves me. Why shouldn't I show my love?'

June, who was clever as well as pretty, was away at college training to be a schoolteacher. It had been considered wiser, long before Walter Symonds was thought of, to keep May at home. She had no particular aptitude for anything and she was useful to her mother about the house. Now, of course, it turned out that she had an aptitude for catching a rich, handsome and successful husband. Then, a month before the wedding, June came home for the summer holidays.

It was all very unfortunate, Mrs Thrace said over and over again. If Walter Symonds had jilted May for some unknown girl, they would have been bitterly indignant, enraged even, and Mr Thrace would have felt old-fashioned longings to apply a horsewhip. But what could anyone say or do when he transferred his affections from the elder daughter to the younger?

May screamed and sobbed and tried to attack June with a knife. 'We're all terribly sorry for you, my darling,' said Mrs Thrace, 'but what can anyone do? You wouldn't marry a man who doesn't love you, would you?'

'He does love me, he does! It's just because she's pretty. She's cast a spell on him. I wish she was dead and then he'd love me again.'

'You mustn't say that, May. It's all very cruel, but you have to face the fact that he's changed his mind. Isn't it better to find out now than later?'

'I would have had him,' said May.

Mrs Thrace blushed. She was shocked to the core.

'I shall never marry now,' said May. 'She's ruined my life and I shall never have anything ever again.'

Walter and June were married, and Walter's father

bought them a big house in Surrey. May stayed at home, being useful to her mother. The war came. Walter went straight into the army, became a captain, a major, finally a colonel. May also went into the army, where she remained a private for five years, working in some catering department. After that, there was nothing for it but to go home to her parents once more.

She never forgave her sister.

'She stole my husband,' she said to her mother.

'He wasn't your husband, May.'

'As good as. You wouldn't forgive a thief who came into your house and stole the most precious thing you had or were likely to have.'

'We're told to forgive those who trespass against us, as we hope to be forgiven.'

'I'm not religious,' said May, and on those occasions when the Symondses came to the Thrace home she took care to be out of it. But she knew all about them – all, that is, except one thing.

Mr and Mrs Thrace were most careful never to speak of June in her presence, so May listened outside the door, and she secretly read all June's letters to her mother. Whenever Walter's name was spoken or mentioned in a letter, she winced and shivered with the pain of it. She knew that they had moved to a much larger house, that they were building up a collection of furniture and pictures. She knew where they went for their holidays and what friends they entertained. But what she was never able to discover was how Walter felt about June. Had he ever really loved her? Had he repented of his choice? May thought that perhaps, after the first flush of infatuation was over, he had come to long for his former love as much as she longed for him. Since she never saw them she could never know, for, however he might feel, Walter couldn't leave June. When you have done what he had done you can't change again. You have to stick it out till death.

It comforted her, it was perhaps the only thing that kept her going, to convince herself that Walter regretted his bargain. If there had been children, what the Victorians called pledges of love...

Sometimes, after a letter had come from June, May would see her mother looked particularly pleased and satisfied. And then, shaking with dread, she would read the letter, terrified to find that June was pregnant. But Mrs Thrace's pleasure and satisfaction must have come from some other source, from some account of Walter's latest coup in court or June's latest party, for no children came and now June was past forty.

Trained for nothing, May worked as canteen supervisor in a women's hostel. She continued to live at home until her parents died. Their deaths took place within six months, Mrs Thrace dying in March and her widower in August. And that was how it happened that May saw Walter again.

At the time of her mother's cremation, May was ill with a virus infection and unable to attend. But she had no way of avoiding her father's funeral. When she saw Walter come into the church a faintness seized her and she huddled against the pew rail, trembling. She covered her face with her hands to make it seem as if she were praying, and when at last she took them away he was beside her. He took her hand and looked into her face. May's eyes met his which were as blue and compelling as ever, and she saw with anguish that he had lost none of his looks but that they had become only more distinguished. She would have liked to die then, holding his hand and gazing into his face.

'Won't you come and speak to your sister, May?' said

Walter in the rich deep voice which charmed juries, struck terror into the hearts of witnesses and won women. 'Shall we let bygones be bygones on this very sad day?'

May shivered. She withdrew her hand and marched to the back of the church. She placed herself as far away from June as she could get, but not too far to observe that it was June who took Walter's arm as they left and not Walter June's, June who looked up to Walter for comfort while his face remained grave and still, June who clung to him while he merely permitted the clinging. It couldn't be that he was behaving like that because she, May, was there. He must hate and despise June as she, with all her heart, hated and despised her still.

But it was at a funeral that they were reconciled. May learnt of Walter's death through reading an announcement of it in a newspaper. And the pain of it was as great as that she had suffered when her mother had told her he wanted to marry June. She sent flowers, an enormous wreath of snow-white roses that cost her half a week's wages. And of course she would go to the funeral, whether June wanted her there or not.

Apparently June did want her. Perhaps she thought the roses were for the living bereaved and not for the dead. She came up to May and put her arms round her, laying her head against her sister's shoulder in misery and despair. May broke their long silence.

'Now you know what it's like to lose him,' she said.

'Oh, May, May, don't be cruel to me now! Don't hold that against me now. Be kind to me now, I've nothing left.'

So May sat beside June, and after the funeral she went back to the house where June had lived with Walter. In saying she had nothing left, June had presumably been referring to emotional rather than material goods. Apart from certain stately homes she had visited on tours, May had never seen anything like the interior of that house.

'I'm going to retire next month,' she said, 'and then I'll be living in what they call a flatlet – one room and a kitchen.'

Two days later there came a letter from June.

'Dearest May, Don't be angry with me for calling you that. You have always been one of my dearest, in spite of what I did and in spite of your hatred of me. I can't be sorry for what I did because so much happiness came of it for me, but I am truly, deeply, sorry that you were the one to suffer. And now, dear May, I want to try to make up to you for what I did, though I know I can never really do that, not now, not after so long. You said you were going to retire and wouldn't be living very comfortably. Will you come and live with me? You can have as many rooms in this house as you want, you are welcome to share everything with me. You will know what I mean when I say I feel that would be just. Please make me happy by saying you forgive me and will come. Always your loving sister, June.'

What did the trick was June saying it would be just. Yes, it would be justice if May could now have some of those good things which were hers by right and which June had stolen from her along with her man. She waited a week before replying and then she wrote: 'Dear June, What you suggest seems a good idea. I have thought about it and I will make my home with you. I have very little personal property, so moving will not be a great headache. Let me know when you want me to come. It is raining again here and very cold. Yours, May.' There was nothing, however, in the letter about forgiveness.

And yet May, sharing June's house, was almost prepared to forgive. For she was learning at last what June's married life had been.

'You can talk about him if you want to,' she had said hungrily on their first evening together. 'If it's going to relieve your feelings, I don't mind.'

'What is there to say except that we were married for forty years and now he's dead?'

'You could show me some of the things he gave you.' May picked up ornaments, gazed at pictures. 'Did he give you that? What about this?'

'They weren't presents. I bought them or he did.'

May couldn't help getting excited. 'I wonder you're not afraid of burglars. This is a proper Aladdin's Cave. Have you got lots of jewellery too?'

'Not much,' said June uncomfortably.

May's eyes were on June's engagement ring, a poor thing of diamond chips in nine carat gold, far less expensive than the ring Walter had given his first love. Of course she had kept hers and Walter, though well off even then, hadn't been rich enough to buy a second magnificent ring within six months of the first. But later, surely ...?

'I should have thought you'd have an eternity ring.'

'Marriage doesn't last for eternity,' said June. 'Let's not talk about it any more.'

May could tell she didn't like talking about it. Soon she shied at mentioning Walter's name and she put away the photographs of him which had stood on the piano and the drawing-room mantelpiece. May wondered if Walter had ever written any letters to his wife. They had seldom been parted, of course, but it would be strange if June had received no letter from him in forty years. The first time June went out alone, May tried to open her desk. It was locked. The drawers of

June's dressing table disclosed a couple of birthday cards with 'Love from Walter' scrawled hastily on them, and the only other written message from her husband June had considered worth keeping May found tucked into a cookery book in the kitchen. It was a note written on the back of a bill, and it read: 'Baker called. I ordered large white for Saturday.'

That night May reread the two letters she had received from Walter during their engagement. Each began, 'Dearest May.' She hadn't looked at them for forty years – she hadn't dared – but now she read them with calm satisfaction. 'Dearest May, This is the first love letter I have ever written. If it isn't much good you must put it down to lack of practice. I miss you a lot and rather wish I hadn't told my parents I would come on this holiday with them ...' 'Dearest May, Thanks for both your letters. Sorry I've taken so long to reply but I feel a bit nervous that my letters don't match up to yours. Still, with luck, we soon shan't have to write to each other because we shan't be separated. I wish you were here with me ...' Poor Walter had been reticent and shy, unable to express his feelings on paper or by word of mouth. But at least he had written love letters to her and not notes about loaves of bread. May decided to start wearing her engagement ring again – on her little finger of course because she could no longer get it over the knuckle of her ring finger. If June noticed she didn't remark on it.

'Was it you or Walter who didn't want children?' May asked.

'Children just didn't come.'

'Walter *must* have wanted them. When he was engaged to me we talked of having three.'

June looked upset but May could have talked of Walter all day long.

'He was only sixty-five,' she said. 'That's young to die these days. You never told me what he died of.'

'Cancer,' said June. 'They operated but he never regained consciousness.'

'Just like mother,' said May. Suppose June had had cancer and had died, what would have happened then? Remembering Walter's tender look and strong handclasp at her father's funeral, May thought he would have married her. She twisted the ring on her little finger. 'You were almost like a second wife, weren't you? It must be a difficult position.'

'I'd much rather not talk about it,' said June, and with her handkerchief to her eyes she left the room.

May was happy. For the first time in forty years she was happy. She busied herself about the house, caring for June's things, dusting and polishing, pausing to look at a picture and reflecting that Walter must often have looked at it. Sometimes she imagined him sitting in this chair or standing by that window, his heart full of regret for what he might have had. And she thought now, while he had been longing for her she, far away, had been crying for him. She never cried now, though June did.

'I'm an old fool, I can't help giving way. You're strong, May, but I'm weak and I miss him so.'

'Didn't I miss him?'

'He was always fond of you. It upset him a lot to think you were unhappy. He often talked about you.' June looked at her piteously. 'You have forgiven me, haven't you, May?'

'As a matter of fact, I have,' said May. She was a little surprised at herself but, yes, she had forgiven June. 'I think you've been punished for what you did.' A loveless marriage, a husband who talked constantly of another woman ...

'I've been punished,' said June and she put her arms round May's neck.

The strong and the weak. May remembered those words when a movement downstairs woke her in the night. She heard footsteps and the sound of a door being forced. It was the burglar she feared and had warned June about, but June would be cowering in her room now, incapable of taking any action.

May put on her dressing gown and went stealthily along the passage to June's room. The bed was empty. She looked out of the window, and the moonlight showed her a car parked on the gravel drive that led down to the lane. A yellower, stronger light streamed from the drawing-room window. A shiver of fear went through her, but she knew she must be strong.

Before she reached the head of the stairs she heard a violent crash as of something heavy yet brittle hurled against a wall. There was a cry from below, footsteps running. May got to the stairs in time to see a slight figure rush across the hall and slam the front door behind him. The car started up.

In his wake he had left a thin trail of blood. May followed the blood trail into the drawing room. June stood by her desk which had been torn open and all its contents scattered on to the table. She was trembling, tearful and laughing with shaky hysteria, pointing to the shards of cut glass that lay everywhere.

'I threw the decanter at him. I hit him and it cut his head and he ran.'

May went up to her. 'Are you all right?'

'He didn't touch me. He pointed that gun at me when I came in, but I didn't care. I couldn't bear to see him searching my desk, getting at all my private things. Wasn't I brave? He didn't get away with anything but a few bits of silver. I hit him and he heard you coming and he panicked. Wasn't I brave, May?'

But May wasn't listening. She was reading the letter which lay open and exposed on top of the paper the burglar had pulled out of the desk. Walter's bold handwriting leapt at her, weakened though it was, enfeebled by his last illness. 'My darling love, It is only a moment since you walked out of the ward, but nevertheless I must write to you. I can't resist an impulse to write now and tell you how happy you have made me in all the years we have been together. If the worst comes to the worst, my darling, and I don't survive the operation, I want you to know you are the only woman I have ever loved ...'

'I wouldn't have thought I'd have had the courage,' said June, 'but perhaps the gun wasn't loaded. He was only a boy. Would you call the police, please, May?'

'Yes,' said May. She picked up the gun.

The police arrived within fifteen minutes. They brought a doctor with them, but June was already dead, shot through the heart at close range.

'We'll get him, Miss Thrace, don't you worry,' said the inspector.

'It was a pity you touched the gun, though. Did it without thinking, I suppose?'

'It was the shock,' said May. 'I've never had a shock like that, not since I was a girl.'

Science fiction

The poet W.H. Auden dismissed science fiction, saying, 'I'm not very interested in other planets. I like them where they are, in the sky.' But sci-fi maestro Brian Aldiss argued that 'the most powerful and compelling theme in science fiction is the fate which overcomes man when he attempts to outdo nature'. The best sci-fi, therefore, holds a mirror not to other worlds, but to our own. The key ingredient may be the question: 'What if . . . ?'

The Forgotten Enemy

by Arthur C. Clarke

The thick furs thudded softly to the ground as Professor Millward jerked himself upright on the narrow bed. This time, he was sure, it had been no dream; the freezing air that rasped against his lungs still seemed to echo with the sound that had come crashing out of the night.

He gathered the furs around his shoulders and listened intently. All was quiet again: from the narrow windows on the western walls long shafts of moonlight played upon the endless rows of books, as they played upon the dead city beneath. The world was utterly still; even in the old days the city would have been silent on such a night, and it was doubly silent now.

With weary resolution Professor Millward shuffled out of bed, and doled a few lumps of coke into the glowing brazier. Then he made his way slowly towards the nearest window, pausing now and then to rest his hand lovingly on the volumes he had guarded all these years.

He shielded his eyes from the brilliant moonlight and peered out into the night. The sky was cloudless: the sound he had heard had not been thunder, whatever it might have been. It had come from the north, and even as he waited it came again.

Distance had softened it, distance and the bulk of the hills that lay beyond London. It did not race across the sky with the wantonness of thunder, but seemed to come from a single point far to the north. It was like no natural sound that he had ever heard, and for a moment he dared to hope again.

Only Man, he was sure, could have made such a sound. Perhaps the dream that had kept him here among these treasures of civilisation for more than twenty years would soon be a dream no longer. Men were returning to England, blasting their way through the ice and snow with the weapons that science had given them before the coming of the Dust. It was strange that they should come by land, and from the north, but he thrust aside any thoughts that would quench the newly kindled flame of hope.

Three hundred feet below, the broken sea of snow-covered roofs lay bathed in the bitter moonlight. Miles away the tall stacks of Battersea Power Station glimmered like thin white ghosts against the night sky. Now that the dome of St Paul's had collapsed beneath the weight of snow, they alone challenged his supremacy.

Professor Millward walked slowly back along the book-shelves, thinking over the plan that had formed in his mind. Twenty years ago he had watched the last helicopters climbing heavily out of Regent's Park, the rotors churning the ceaselessly falling snow. Even then, when the silence had closed around him, he could not bring himself to believe that the North had been abandoned for ever. Yet already he had waited a whole generation, among the books to which he had dedicated his life.

In those early days he had sometimes heard, over the radio which was his only contact with the South, of the struggle to colonise the now-temperate lands of the Equator. He did not know the outcome of that far-off battle, fought with desperate skill in the dying jungles and across deserts that had already felt the first touch of snow. Perhaps it had failed; the radio had been silent now for fifteen years or more. Yet if men and machines were indeed returning from the north – of all directions – he might again be able to hear their voices as they spoke to one another and to the lands from which they had come.

Professor Millward left the University building perhaps a dozen times a year, and then only through sheer necessity. Over the past two decades he had collected everything he needed from the shops in the Bloomsbury area, for in the final exodus vast supplies of stocks had been left behind through lack of transport. In many ways, indeed, his life could be called luxurious: no professor of English literature had ever been clothed in such garments as those he had taken from an Oxford Street furrier's.

The sun was blazing from a cloudless sky as he shouldered his pack and unlocked the massive gates. Even ten years ago packs of starving dogs had hunted in this area, and though he had seen none for years he was still cautious and always carried a revolver when he went into the open.

The sunlight was so brilliant that the reflected glare hurt his eyes; but it was almost wholly lacking in heat. Although the belt of cosmic dust through which the Solar System was now passing had made little difference to the sun's brightness, it had robbed it of all strength. No one knew whether the world would swim out into the warmth again in ten or a thousand years, and civilisation had fled southwards in search of lands where the word 'summer' was not an empty mockery.

The latest drifts had packed hard, and Professor Millward had little difficulty in making the journey to Tottenham Court Road. Sometimes it had taken him hours of floundering through the snow, and one year he had been sealed in his great concrete watch-tower for nine months.

He kept away from the houses with their dangerous burdens of snow and their Damoclean icicles, and went north until he came to the shop he was seeking. The words above the shattered windows were still bright: 'Jenkins & Sons. Radio and Electrical. Television A Speciality.'

Some snow had drifted through a broken section of roofing, but the little upstairs room had not altered since his last visit a dozen years ago. The all-wave radio still stood on the table, and empty tins scattered on the floor spoke mutely of the lonely hours he had spent here before all hope had died. He wondered if he must go through the same ordeal again.

Professor Millward brushed the snow from the copy of *The Amateur Radio Handbook for 1965*, which had taught him what little he knew about wireless. The test-meters and batteries were still lying in their half-remembered places, and to his relief some of the batteries still held their charge. He searched through the stock until he had built up the necessary power supplies, and checked the radio as well as he could. Then he was ready.

It was a pity that he could never send the manufacturers the testimonial they deserved. The faint 'hiss' from the speaker brought back memories of the BBC, of the nine o'clock news and symphony concerts, of all the things he had taken for granted in a world that was gone like a dream. With scarcely controlled impatience he ran across the wave-bands, but everywhere there was nothing save that omnipresent hiss. That was disappointing, but no more: he remembered that the real test would come at night. In the meantime he would forage among the surrounding shops for anything that might be useful.

It was dusk when he returned to the little room. A hundred miles above his head, tenuous and invisible, the Heaviside Layer would be expanding outwards toward the stars as the sun went down. So it had done every evening for millions of years, and for half a century only, Man had used it for his own purposes, to reflect around the world his messages of hate or peace, to echo with trivialities or to sound with music once called immortal.

Slowly, with infinite patience, Professor Millward began to traverse the shortwave bands that a generation ago had been a babel of shouting voices and stabbing morse. Even as he listened, the faint hope that he had dared to cherish began to fade within him. The city itself was no more silent than the once-crowded oceans of ether. Only the faint crackle of thunderstorms half the world away broke the intolerable stillness. Man had abandoned his latest conquest.

Soon after midnight the batteries faded out. Professor Millward did not have the heart to search for more, but curled up in his furs and fell into a troubled sleep. He got what consolation he could from the thought that if he had not proved his theory, he had not disproved it either.

The heatless sunlight was flooding the lonely white road when he began the homeward journey. He was very tired, for he had slept little, and his sleep had been broken by the recurring fantasy of rescue.

The silence was suddenly broken by the distant thunder that came rolling over the white roofs. It came – there could be no doubt now – from beyond the northern hills that had once been London's playground. From the buildings on either side little avalanches of snow went swishing out into the wide street; then the silence returned.

Professor Millward stood motionless, weighing, considering, analysing. The sound had been too long-drawn out to be an ordinary explosion – he was dreaming again – it was nothing less than the distant thunder of an atomic bomb, burning and blasting away the snow a million tons at a time. His hopes revived, and the disappointments of the night began to fade.

That momentary pause almost cost him his life. Out of a sidestreet something huge and white moved suddenly into his field of vision. For a moment his mind refused to accept the reality of what he saw: then the paralysis left him and he fumbled desperately for his futile revolver. Padding towards him across the snow, swinging its head from side to side with a hypnotic, serpentine motion, was a huge polar bear.

He dropped his belongings and ran, floundering over the snow towards the nearest buildings. Providentially the Underground entrance was only fifty feet away. The steel grille was closed, but he remembered breaking the lock many years ago. The temptation to look back was almost intolerable, for he could hear nothing to tell how near his pursuer was. For one frightful moment the iron lattice resisted his numbed fingers. Then it yielded reluctantly and he forced his way through the narrow opening.

Out of his childhood there came a sudden incongruous memory of an albino ferret he had once seen weaving its body ceaselessly across the wire netting of its cage. There was the same reptile grace in the monstrous shape, almost twice as high as a man, that reared itself in baffled fury against the grille. The metal bowed but did not yield beneath the pressure; then the bear dropped to the ground, grunted softly, and padded away. It slashed once or twice at the fallen

33

haversack, scattering a few tins of food into the snow, and vanished as silently as it had come.

A very shaken Professor Millward reached the University three hours later, after moving in short bounds from one refuge to the next. After all these years he was no longer alone in the city. He wondered if there were other visitors, and that same night he knew the answer. Just before dawn he heard, quite distinctly, the cry of a wolf from somewhere in the direction of Hyde Park.

By the end of the week he knew that the animals of the North were on the move. Once he saw a reindeer running southward pursued by a pack of silent wolves, and sometimes in the night there were sounds of deadly conflict. He was amazed that so much life still existed in the white wilderness between London and the Pole. Now something was driving it southward, and the knowledge brought him a mounting excitement. He did not believe that these fierce survivors would flee from anything save Man.

The strain of waiting was beginning to affect Professor Millward's mind, and for hours he would sit in the cold sunlight, his furs wrapped round him, dreaming of rescue and thinking of the way in which men might be returning to England. Perhaps an expedition had come from North America across the Atlantic ice. It might have been years upon its way. But why had it come so far north? His favourite theory was that the Atlantic ice-packs were not safe enough for heavy traffic farther to the south.

One thing, however, he could not explain to his satisfaction. There had been no air reconnaissance; it was hard to believe that the art of flight had been lost so soon.

Sometimes he would walk along the ranks of books,

whispering now and then to a well-loved volume. There were books here that he had not dared to open for years, they reminded him so poignantly of the past. But now, as the days grew longer and brighter he would sometimes take down a volume of poetry and reread his old favourites. Then he would go to the tall windows and shout the magic words over the rooftops, as if they would break the spell that had gripped the world.

It was warmer now, as if the ghosts of lost summers had returned to haunt the land. For whole days the temperature rose above freezing, while in many places flowers were breaking through the snow. Whatever was approaching from the north was nearer, and several times a day that enigmatic roar would go thundering over the city, sending the snow sliding upon a thousand roofs.

There were strange, grinding undertones that Professor Millward found baffling and even ominous. At times it was almost as if he were listening to the clash of mighty armies, and sometimes a mad but dreadful thought came into his mind and would not be dismissed. Often he would wake in the night and imagine he heard the sound of mountains moving to the sea.

So the summer wore away, and as the sound of that distant battle drew steadily nearer Professor Millward was the prey of ever more violent alternating hopes and fears. Although he saw no more wolves or bears – they seemed to have fled southward – he did not risk leaving the safety of his fortress. Every morning he would climb to the highest window of the tower and search the northern horizon with field glasses. But all he ever saw was the stubborn retreat of the snows above Hampstead, as they fought their bitter rearguard action against the sun.

His vigil ended with the last days of the brief summer. The grinding thunder in the night had been nearer than ever before, but there was still nothing to hint at its real distance from the city. Professor Millward felt no premonition as he climbed to the narrow window and raised his binoculars to the northern sky.

As a watcher from the walls of some threatened fortress might have seen the first sunlight glinting on the spears of an advancing army, so in that moment Professor Millward knew the truth. The air was crystal-clear, and the hills were sharp and brilliant against the cold blue of the sky. They had lost almost all their snow. Once he would have rejoiced, but it meant nothing now.

Overnight, the enemy he had forgotten had conquered the last defences and was preparing for the final onslaught. As he saw that deadly glitter along the crest of the doomed hills, Professor Millward understood at last the sound he had heard advancing for so many months. It was little wonder he had dreamed of mountains on the march.

Out of the North, their ancient home, returning in triumph to the lands they had once possessed, the glaciers had come again.

Horror

As writer Lisa Tuttle reminds us: 'Fear is a basic and universal emotion, usually something we try to avoid, but not always'. The best horror stories – whether in books or on screen – show us our worst nightmares. Perhaps knowing that they are fiction allows us to respond to them with a mix of terror and delight. Key ingredients: ordinary people in ordinary settings, but then something or someone begins deliberately to break the rules – to do the unthinkable . . .

Getting Away from It All

by Ann Walsh

The rats came the first night. She had seen their signs in the cabin when she unlocked the door, and, trying to hide her own revulsion, had persuaded the children to sweep up the droppings and tufts of cotton pulled from the upholstered couch. By the time she had, according to the real estate lady's instructions, activated the propane appliances, pumped up the cistern that supplied running water, and disposed of the two full saucers of rat poison, the girls had finished their attempt at sweeping. It was clean enough for now, she thought. Tomorrow she would sweep again, and mop the floor with a strong bleach solution. Exhausted by the long drive and the search for the isolated cabin that she had rented for the summer, she tucked the girls firmly into their sleeping bags in one bedroom, settled herself in the other, and fell into a deep, dreamless sleep.

She should have realised, she told herself the next morning, she should have realised that the rats would come back. The groceries she had left stacked on the kitchen counter were scattered on the floor; loose macaroni mixing with rice, sugar, and corn flakes. Every box, every bag, every item she had so carefully packed had been damaged in some way. Even less edible items – soap, pepper, paper towels – had been savaged, and fresh black droppings lay over everything like a satanic snowfall.

She cleaned up and, by the time the children woke, the kitchen showed no sign of the invasion. Everything was stored in the oven, the fridge, or sealer jars she had found in a cupboard, and she had discovered a large box of rat poison and refilled the saucers.

The cabin had been abandoned for several years, which was why the rent was within her single-parent budget. A faded 'For Sale' sign hung crookedly on a tree outside, mutely pleading for new owners. It was not far from a small town, but the access road, eleven miles of deeply rutted, treacherous trail, had probably discouraged buyers.

Around the cabin the weeds were waist high, and she had to carry the four-year-old as they struggled down to the beach. A patch of scorched earth marked a firepit, and a picnic table stood nearby, almost hidden in a thick stand of purple fireweed.

'Mummy?' Jenny's voice, usually strident with first-grade exuberance, was soft, timid. 'Do we *have* to stay in this place? I don't think I like it here.'

'Nonsense, Jen. It's just overgrown, lonely. No one has taken care of it for a long time. We'll clear a nice path down to the beach – see, there *is* a bit of a path under the weeds – then it will be easier for you to walk. We can build a campfire tonight and have hot dogs and marshmallows. It will be *fun*!' She smiled at the child, wondering why her own voice had sounded so loud and harsh.

The beach was beautiful; sandy and shallow for a long way out and nestled in a small cove that kept the water calm and warm. While the children splashed and searched for frogs, she began clearing the trail with a rusty, but still serviceable sickle she found near the picnic table.

Once, stopping work to wipe the sweat from her eyes

and to check on the children, she glanced up at the hillside behind her and saw, almost hidden among tall cedars, the dark bulk of another, larger, cabin.

Curious, for no one had mentioned a second place close by, she called to the girls to stay out of the water until she came back, and pushed through the deep undergrowth on the hillside towards the hidden cabin.

It was large, built of grey-weathered logs, and surrounded by a wooden porch with a low railing. As she got closer, she could see that it was obviously deserted, and had been for a long time. The windows were boarded over with plywood, the steps to the front porch were pushed askew by saplings that nudged the foundation, and two solid planks were nailed, cross-like, over the front door. Oddly disappointed, she turned, and began the downward climb. As she walked, she realised why the large cabin had been built so far away from the water. The view was spectacular. She could see far across the lake, around a bend in the shore, to where a solitary mountain, still snow-capped in July, reared distantly through the heat haze. Below her the lake threw off slices of sunlight, and she could see her children digging intently in the sand. Of her own cabin, she glimpsed only the roof and her bedroom window through the trees.

In the evening, sunburned and exhausted, the girls again crawled into bed early. She made herself a cup of tea and with it walked down the now cleared path to the beach, admiring her handiwork. She stayed until the sun began to set, watching the coloured rays slant off the water, then, tired herself, she made her way back up the trail.

When she reached the cabin, both children were crying. She ran to their room, stopping abruptly as a large grey rat sitting between the two beds slowly turned, stared at her for a moment with basalt eyes, then scurried between her legs and out the door.

She reassured the children, set out yet another saucer of poison, and went to bed. That night she dreamed that she heard music.

Slowly, the cabin became home. The rats stayed away, although the poisoned bait seemed untouched. The sickle and an old push-mower revealed a tiny lawn, and the appearance of pansies alerted her to the presence of a flower bed edged with white-painted rocks. She took out several years' growth of weeds and discovered other perennials – pinks, day lilies and a clump of flowering poppies. Someone had once spent a great deal of time in this place, she thought. The propane stove, fridge and hot water heater, the fully operational bathroom and ingenious water supply, the flower beds and the pleasant, solid furniture, all suggested a 'home' rather than just a summer cabin. A home that someone had loved, but left. 'Why?' she wondered, but quickly pushed the thought aside. Now it was her home; at least for a while. The children were happy; their bodies becoming tanned, their hair sun-streaked. The treasures of lake and forest, new to city children – minnows, frogs, chipmunks and the small kayak they had found, were keeping them cheerfully occupied. She was happy, too, she realised. Content. At peace.

But by the end of the first week in the cabin she was no longer sleeping well. The music that she heard in her dreams became louder, more persistent. There were party sounds too – the clink of glasses, distant bursts of laughter, sudden spatterings of conversations that she couldn't quite understand. Her dreams were always the same; she was lying in the narrow cot in the cabin and angrily listening to the sounds of a party to which she was not invited.

Then one night she realised that she *wasn't* asleep, *wasn't* dreaming! She sat up, fully awake, and listened. The music still played, the faint voices laughed. She went to the bedroom window, pushed aside the curtain, and stared out into the night. The big cabin on the hill glowed with light. It streamed through the large front windows, over the porch, touching the cedars with colour. Shadows moved against the windows, and the music seemed louder.

Puzzled, she let the curtain fall back into place and went into the kitchen. She lit the lamps, made tea, and tried to laugh at herself and her sudden fear. The owners of the large cabin had come back and she, being so involved with the children, the lake, the flowers, hadn't noticed them arriving, that was all. But, wouldn't she or the children have heard a car? Several cars in fact? And there *was* no road up the hill to the big cabin. Well, maybe there was another road, one she hadn't noticed. They could have come that way, perhaps.

But...the plywood had been removed from the windows, the front door was open, unbarred. Surely she would have heard hammering, shouts, the noises of opening a house that has been abandoned for a long time.

She stayed there in the bright kitchen until the dawn came, listening to the sounds that faded with the growing light. When the sun dimmed the propane lights and tentatively reached across the room, she stood up and went outside. Uneasily, but with a growing sense of anticipation, she made her way through the long, early morning shadows, up the hill, towards the large, now silent, cabin.

Nothing had changed since she had last seen it. The boarded-over windows and doors, the saplings and weeds pushing against the porch and stairs, and the thick, undisturbed underbush on all sides were just as she had first seen them.

After that, she didn't try to sleep, but spent all her nights in the kitchen, turning the pages of a book, drinking tea, trying not to listen to the voices she knew she could not be hearing. The twelfth night she heard them call her name.

The tourists were American, elderly, and kind. They pulled their big car on to the shoulder of the country road and spoke to the two bedraggled children who stood there, holding hands and trying not to cry.

'Mummy went away,' said the oldest, rubbing at her eyes with a scratched, sunburned hand. 'For two whole days. We got scared so we walked to the road.'

'We got losted,' said the small one. 'And see, a big rat in the cabin bit me. But I didn't cry.'

She held out her arm, proudly. The tourists looked at each other, their eyes wide with some unspeakable thought, then bundled the children into the car, turned around, and drove hurriedly back to the town they had just passed.

For on the child's arm was the perfect imprint of a vicious bite – two deep half-circles, the unmistakable mark left only by human teeth.

Travel writing

·····························

Famous travel writer Eric Newby asked why people travel and concluded: 'To find out what is over the seas, over the hills and far away, round the corner, over the garden wall.' Travel writers frequently return home thinking not only of their journeys, but of themselves and how they have changed. The genre often, therefore, reads like exotic autobiography. Key ingredients: details of people and places, a first-person narrative style (*I* rather than *she* or *he*), a desire to entertain and inform . . .

Among the Rhinos

from *Speak to the Earth*

by Vivienne de Watteville

Vivienne de Watteville had been on several hazardous trips to
see African wildlife during the 1930s. In this extract she
returns to Kenya, hoping to film some of the more dangerous
animals.

Then, suddenly, toiling upwards through trees and
creepers, I came out on to an open crest, and there
before me, lifting its head above the forest, was the
bare, grey summit. It might have been three hours away
and it might have been thirty: all depended upon what
lay between those intervening ridges suffocating under
the tangled green barriers of forest. But to the eye it
looked attainable, and the more I looked, the more it
lured me on. It was no use discussing the possibilities
with the men, and I took a high hand.

'The mountain is near enough,' I said, 'we'll follow
the crest,' but I dared not meet Mohamed's eye, nor
did I glance at him.

Sometimes one guide led, sometimes the other, and
when they flagged, or cast about, I struck ahead. But all
at once it was borne in upon me that their resistance
and also that of the jungle itself had both given out at
the same time. Finding that I was not to be put off they
had now cheerfully accepted the position, and put their
interest in what lay ahead. As for the jungle, we had left
the worst of it behind, and the ridge brought us out
into the daylight clear above it. Following one ridge to

the next, with occasional drops into the forest, we climbed a straight and broad path which was hemmed in on either side by dense hedges of greenery.

It was paved all the way with the droppings of rhino, buffalo and elephant. I was ahead and walking along with my eyes bent on the spoor, when I came to a grey boulder lying across the path. I was in the act of walking round it when it suddenly heaved itself up beside me with the terrifying snort of a rhino. I recoiled and leapt backwards, while the rhino (who was presumably facing the other way) tore off in the opposite direction. This is only conjecture; for the instant the boulder sprang to life, I did not wait for a second glance but turned and bolted, colliding with the man behind me, who also turned and ran for his life shouting 'Faru! faru!' (rhino) and in the twinkling of an eye we had scattered like chaff.

The rhino had disappeared, and the forest gradually settled back into silence. One by one, with hearts still beating with fright, we stole out of our several retreats and back to the path.

I suppose that the boys were now worked up to the adventure, or that they had hopes of finding more ivory, for none of them thought of using this as a pretext for going home before worse befell. Still out of breath, they laughed over the scare as each contributed some detail to our comically expeditious flight. But as I started off again, now a trifle daunted and very much on the alert, I began to think that losing the way was a minor evil compared with nearly falling over a sleeping rhino. I was trespassing in a sanctuary where no human being (according to the natives) had ever set foot before, and I could not tell but what there might be plenty more rhino ahead. The forest was ominously silent, and everything pointed to its being unusually full of big and possibly dangerous game. If any of them took it into their heads to charge, and casualties resulted, the blame would be mine for exposing my men to undue risk. It was an unpleasant thought and responsibility began to sit so heavily upon my shoulders that I almost wished that I had given in to the boys an hour back, and left the forest alone.

The rhino, very naturally, had been annoyed at having his sleep so rudely disturbed; and since the path was the only place where a rhino could bask in the sun, the path was obviously a dangerous one to walk, and other sleeping rhino (or buffalo) might be less good-natured.

I was debating within myself whether I was at all justified in going on, when sure enough I detected another grey cumbersome shape above the grass-stalks ahead. It was only a few yards off, but I trained the glasses on it to make certain, and they showed up clearly the grey corrugations of a rhino's hide. I retreated on tiptoe and held a consultation with the boys. A detour was made impossible by the thickness of the jungle on either hand, but Lembogi, always the resourceful one of the party, said that if we retired to safety down-wind, he would climb a tree, wake the rhino by throwing sticks at him, and try to drive him away.

The reader may well wonder why I did not seize this golden opportunity myself, and (with the wind blowing so true) nothing would have been easier than to have crept up to the sleeping rhino and scratched him behind his ears. He might have loved it (and introduced me to the whole forest as a reward) but on the other hand if he hadn't, my chances for experiment would have been for ever curtailed. This would always be the difficulty, for when chances came I did not dare.

So Lembogi threw sticks and bits of caked mud at

him till he awoke, and with many surprised and indignant snorts he took himself off, and we continued on our way.

Each time I hoped that we were on the final crest I would come to another disheartening drop. Mohamed urged me afresh to turn back, saying we should be benighted. I minded very little if we were, for it would hurt none of us; we had matches and could make a fire. The more work I put into that climb, the less I could relinquish it. It is one thing to come home dead-beat but successful, and quite another to be defeated after all; not only that, but I could never get the boys to face it again, and even I was not over-keen on a third venture.

Finally, it was the boys themselves who pointed to the summit and said that it was not very far.

Enviously I admired the way they could climb. As for me, I had put all my energies into the lead when it had been necessary, and now, under the burning midday sun beating fiercely down between thunderclouds, I was badly spent; my knees trembled as I panted up through the reeling boulders. We rested a little, and Asani pointed (as I thought) into a treetop at 'a bird that makes a noise like a motor-car'. I scanned the tree vainly for some strange kind of hooting vulture, when I heard the unmistakable throb of an engine, and picked up a black speck in the sky. I looked at it with profound disgust. Artistically, dramatically, from every point of view, its appearance was ill-timed, not to say tactless. Just as I was blazing the unknown trail, to find I was being actually looked down upon was sheer anticlimax. The fact that the aeroplane was ten miles off was only very mildly consoling. 'But at least,' I thought, 'he can't land on the summit'; and I pushed on.

At last I climbed above the forest zone, passing

beneath the last outposts – stunted trees ragged with beard-moss in whose chequered shade lay a carpet of tiny peas (a kind of vetch with a leaf like wood sorrel, probably the *Parechetus communis*) whose blossoms were a lovely transparent blue. Above them flitted miniature blue butterflies, as though the petals themselves had taken wing.

Heath and boulders rose up against the flying clouds and deep blue sky. I waded through billowing masses of white flowering shrubs, and beyond, all the ground was decked gold and blue and purple with flowers. There must have been fifty different kinds (possibly far more) and one I have never seen anywhere before or since clung to the rock in profusion like a blue mist. It had velvet purplish leaves and clusters of little powdery blue flowers like down, with a sprinkling of golden stamens.

This part of the mountain was a paradise of wild flowers. The Alps in the full glory of springtide could not have unfolded anything more tender or more vivid; indeed, the intensity of those burning blues and golds nodding in the hot scented air against the almost sapphire sky and the shimmering pillars of cloud produced an effect that was peculiarly Alpine. I lingered there, willy-nilly, promising myself that I would return another day when I should have plenty of time. How often one bribes oneself with these false promises to return to something specially entrancing glimpsed on the road to something else!

The top, when at last I reached it was, after all, not really the top, and beyond a dipping saddle another granite head still frowned down upon me.

But meanwhile, below me the south side disclosed a grassy depression girt about by the two summits and bare granite screes; and amid that desolation the grass stretched so green and rural that you had looked there for shepherds with their flocks. Instead of which, on the far side of a quaking bog, I saw – grey among the grey slabs – two rhino.

Leaving Lembogi, Kabechi and the old guide behind, I took Asani with the cameras and ran down the slope, crossed the bog and climbed up the far side. Mohamed was to follow at a short distance, on account of the clatter of his boots on the rocks. I drew to within forty yards of the rhino, yet they still looked like a couple of grey boulders as they browsed off an isolated patch of sere grass. The bleached stalks bowing before the wind alone gave a flicker of life to that adamantine expanse of stone.

The wind had risen to a tearing gale, and nosing straight into it I approached the rhino somewhat down-hill. There was no chance of this steady blow jumping round to betray me, and it was strong enough to carry away any sound of my footsteps. Precaution was there-fore unnecessary, and I walked boldly up to them. Just how close I was, it is hard to say; but I felt that I could have flipped a pebble at them, and I noted subcon-sciously that the eye of the one nearest me was not dark brown as I had imagined it, but the colour of sherry.

And the experience has left me in some doubt whether a rhino has such poor sight as is commonly believed. Perhaps they heard the clicking of the cinema camera. This may have given the nearer one my direc-tion, and then my coat or the brim of my hat flapping in the wind possibly caught his eye. At any rate, his ears pricked up, his champing jaws were held in suspense, and that little pale eye was very definitely focused straight upon me.

He lifted his head, trying to catch the wind. It told him nothing, but he now came deliberately towards me, nose to the ground and horn foremost, full of suspicion. I pressed the button and tried to keep a steady hand. This was not easy; for a rhino seen through the finder of a small cinema camera looks remote, and it is only when you take the camera down to make sure, that you are horribly startled to see how near he really is. In the finder I saw his tail go up, and knew that he was on the point of charging. Though it was the impression of a fraction of a second, it was unforgettable. He was standing squarely upon a flat boulder that raised him like a pedestal, and he seemed to tower up rugged and clear-cut as a monument against the flying clouds.

Such a chance could never possibly occur again, and the magnificence of that picture for the moment blinded me to all else. I had done better to bolt then, while he was still hesitating. I read the danger signal, yet in a kind of trance of excitement I still held the camera against my forehead. Then Mohamed fired a shot over the rhino's head to scare him, and I turned and fled for my very life.

The rhino was only momentarily taken aback. Before I had time to skip out of his sight he had made up his mind to charge me. The angry thunder of his snort, mingled with a screech like an engine blowing off steam, lent me wings. When I dared throw a glance over my shoulder I saw that both rhino were bearing down upon me with frightening speed. The boys had had a start of me, and as I raced after them across the vistas of stone bare as asphalt without a blade of cover anywhere, conviction swept over me that this time the game was up.

Though I ran and ran as I had never run in my life before, and my heart pounded in my ears and my lungs stiffened with the pain of drawing breath, time went suddenly into slow motion. Each step was weighted with lead; I wanted to fly over the ground and, as in some horrid nightmare, I felt as though I were scarcely moving.

The rhino were swiftly gaining upon me; their furious snorts overtook me on the wings of the gale. The boys, on the other hand, had disappeared as though the earth had swallowed them. I made one more desperate spurt and then, as I realised the utter futility of it, a fold in the hillside opened to receive me also. I tumbled headlong down a little cliff and landed on a ledge of heather.

The rhino would never face this drop even if they looked over and saw me. I glanced up apprehensively, but there was no sign of them.

In this sheltered place there was not a sound, and even the wind had dropped. With a thankful heart I stretched myself face downward on the heather, and panted as though I could never get a complete lungful of air again, while waves of crimson and orange rushed and throbbed before my eyes.

The boys climbed up to me (they had landed farther down) and seeing Mohamed's lugubrious expression of disapproval I quickly put my word in first.

'That,' said I, 'is the best picture I have ever taken!' And though unable at once to control my trembling fingers, I turned my attention to the intricate business of changing the film. Asani, taking his cue from me, stoutly declared he had never seen anything like the way the rhino had stood out on that rock; and the three Masai, who had witnessed the whole thing from the other side of the bog, now joined us and gave their version. Even at the time, I had been dimly aware that they were yelling with excitement as though they were cheering the winner of the Grand National. It must have been worth watching, and the pity was that there had not been a second photographer.

During their graphic recounting of what had happened, even Mohamed began to unbend and smile. Congratulations rained down upon his modest head, as well they ought, for his well-timed shot had undoubtedly saved my life.

As I was busy with the camera and listened to their talk, I too began quietly to enjoy myself. There is nothing like an escape to give you the feeling of exhilaration. The pleasant glow of it was stealing over me when I made a crushing discovery. In changing the film I found that I had overshot the end by fully six feet. This meant that the rhino's mad rush and the dramatic moment when he had stood silhouetted against the sky, were recorded on nothing but blind, red paper. The disappointment was bitter, so bitter that there were no words for it. The boys still talked of the marvellous picture, and I had not the heart to undeceive them.

Journeys by Railway

from *Stranger on a Train: The Pleasures of Railways*

by Paul Theroux

There are two sorts of people who like trains, and I am neither. The first is the railway buff, for whom trains are toys. With the mind of a child and the constitution of a night-watchman, he has been elderly in that pipe-stuffing British way since he started to smoke; he enjoys running his thumb along the coachwork and jotting down engine numbers on a greasy note–pad, and though he smiles bizarrely when the whistle blows, he doesn't climb aboard: he is going nowhere. . . .

It is well-known that the train is the last word in truth drugs. All the world's airlines have failed to inspire what one choo-choo train has: the dramas of 'The Orient Express' and a whole library of railway masterpieces. A rail journey is virtually the only occasion in travel on which complete strangers bare their souls, because the rail passenger – the calmest of travellers – has absolutely nothing to lose. He has more choices than anyone else in motion: unlike the air-traveller strapped in his chair like a candidate for electrocution, he can stroll, enjoy the view and sleep in privacy in a horizontal position – he can travel, as the natives do, the six thousand miles from Nakhodka to Moscow, in his pyjamas; unlike the person on shipboard, he can restore his eyes with landscape, eat whenever he chooses and never know the ghastly jollity of group games – and he can get off whenever he likes. He can remain anonymous, adopt a disguise, or spend the five days from Istanbul to Tehran canoodling in his couchette. The train offers the maximum of opportunity with the minimum of risk. A train journey is *travel*; everything else – planes especially – is *transfer*, your journey beginning when you arrive....

I began by saying that there are two sorts of people who like trains – the railway buff and the joy-rider. There are also two sorts of travellers.

There are those whom we instantly recognise as clinging to the traditional virtues of travel, the people who endure a kind of alienation and panic in foreign parts for the after-taste of having sampled new scenes. On the whole travel at its best is rather comfortless, but travel is never easy: you get very tired, you get lost, you get your feet wet, you get little co-operation, and – if it is to have any value at all – you go alone. Homesickness is part of this kind of travel. In these circumstances, it is possible to make interesting discoveries about oneself and one's surroundings. Travel has less to do with distance than with insight; it is, very often, a way of seeing. The other day I was walking through London and saw an encampment of gypsies on a patch of waste ground – the caravans, the wrecked cars, the junked machines, the rubbish; and children wandering through this cityscape in metal. This little area had a 'foreign' look to me. I was curious, but I didn't investigate – because, like many other people, I suppress the desire to travel in my own city. I think we do this because we don't want to risk dangerous or unpleasant or disappointing experiences in the place in which we live: we don't want to know too much. And we don't want to be exposed. As everyone knows, it is wrong to be too conspicuously curious – much better to leave this for foreign places. All these are the characteristics of a person with a travelling mind.

The second group of travellers has only appeared in numbers in the past twenty years. For these people travel, paradoxically, is an experience of familiar things; it is travel that carries with it the illusion of immobility. It is the going to a familiar airport and being strapped into a seat and held captive for a number of hours – immobile; then arriving at an almost identical airport, being whisked to a hotel so fast it is not like movement at all; and the hotel and the food here are identical to the hotel and the food in the city one has just left. Apart from the sunshine or the lack of, there is nothing new. This is all tremendously reassuring and effortless; indeed, it is possible to go from – say – London to Singapore and not experience the feeling of having travelled anywhere.

For many years, in the past, this was enjoyed by the rich. It is wrong to call it tourism, because businessmen also travel this way; and many people, who believe themselves to be travellers, object to being called tourists. The luxury travellers of the past set an example for the package tourists of today: What was the Grand Tour but a gold-plated package tour, giving the illusion of gaining experience and seeing the world?

In this sort of travel, you take your society with you: your language, your food, your styles of hotel and service. It is of course the prerogative of rich nations – America, western Europe, and Japan.

It has had a profound effect on our view of the world. It has made real travel greatly sought after and somewhat rare. And I think it has caused a resurgence in travel writing.

As everyone knows, travel is very unsettling, and it

can be quite hazardous and worrying. One way of overcoming this anxiety is to travel packaged in style: luxury is a great remedy for the alienation of travel. What helps calm us is a reminder of stability and protection – and what the average package tourist looks for in foreign surroundings is familiar sights. This person goes to China or Peru and wants to feel at home. Is this a contradiction? I suppose it is, but we must remember that in the past the very rich went from castle to castle or court to court; from the court of George III in London to the court of The Son of Heaven in Peking. It is much the same among certain travellers today. I was once in Siberia, and I recall an Australian saying to me in a complaining way, 'It's *cold* here!' In Peru an American woman said to me, 'I hate these hills – they're too steep.' We were in the Andes. And not long ago, in China, a woman said to me, 'I've been all around the world – Madagascar, the Galapagos Islands, Arabia, everywhere – and I didn't walk. I never walk. I hate to walk. I never go to places where I have to walk. But I've been everywhere.'

This is actually quite extraordinary. For that woman, travel is a sedentary activity. She has been carried across the world. She is the true armchair traveller.

It is easy to laugh at her, but her kind of travelling is very popular. Travel nowadays is seen to be a form of repose: most people you see in travel posters are lying down in the sunshine, or sleeping in a lounge chair, or just sitting. In a sense, Abroad is where you don't have to do anything but loaf. I realise that a great confusion has arisen because we regard *travel* and a *vacation* as interchangeable. But really there is no connection at all between being alone in upcountry Honduras and, on the other hand, eating fish and chips in Spain. For a person with two weeks' vacation, travel – in its traditional sense – would be unthinkable; which is why parts of Spain have become Blackpool with sunshine – it's more restful that way. I don't blame people for craving that, but I do object when it is regarded as travel....

The interest in travel today, which is passionate, arises out of the fact that there is a form of travel prevalent that is now very easy – people want to find an antidote for the immobility that mass tourism has produced; people want to believe that somewhere, somehow, it is still very dangerous, bizarre, anxiety-making and exotic to travel, that one can still make discoveries in a glorious solitary way. Mock-travel has produced a huge interest in clumsy, old-fashioned travel, with its disgusting food and miseries and long nights. It has also given rise to a lively interest in travel literature, and the affirmation that the world is still large and strange and, thank God, full of empty places that are nothing like home.

Biography

Writer Mark Twain said that 'Biographies are but the clothes and buttons of man – the biography of the man himself cannot be written.' Like many famous people, he was suspicious of those who wanted to write about his life. Yet sales of biographies show that readers love to learn about the lives of other people – celebrities, royalty, people of achievement, notorious criminals, and people of the past. Key ingredients: a writer's fascination with her or his subject, facts and details from the subject's life, a third-person narrative style (*she* or *he* rather than *I*), a wish to put a person's life into some kind of order . . .

Dahl, Roald

CD-ROM Encyclopaedia: Microsoft Encarta

Dahl, Roald (1919–1990), British writer of novels, short stories, and film scripts, but best known for his children's books. He was born in Llandaff, Wales, and educated at Repton, a boarding school for boys. His harsh treatment while a student there led him later to write stories about cruelty and revenge. Deciding not to enter a university, Dahl joined the Shell Oil Company in 1933, worked in Tanganyika from 1937 to 1939, enlisted in the Royal Air Force (RAF) at the start of World War II (1939–1945), and served as a fighter pilot and as an air attaché in Washington, D.C. During those years he published his RAF adventures in the *Saturday Evening Post* and wrote his first book, *The Gremlins* (1943), which became a motion picture in 1984. A collection of short stories, *Someone Like You* (1953), became a best-seller and was followed by *Kiss, Kiss* (1959), which firmly established Dahl as a serious writer of fiction. *Switch Bitch* (1974), another work of adult fiction, continued Dahl's tradition of morbid, eerie tales for adults.

Dahl was the author of 19 children's books, the best known of which were *James and the Giant Peach* (1961) and *Charlie and the Chocolate Factory* (1964), which was made into a movie in 1971. *Fantastic Mr Fox* (1970) and *The BFG* (1982) are more recent children's books. He also wrote a number of film scripts, including *You Only*

Live Twice (1967) and *Chitty Chitty Bang Bang* (1968), both adapted from Ian Fleming novels. Dahl wrote two autobiographies, *Boy* (1984) and *Going Solo* (1986). He was married to American actress Patricia Neal, whom he helped to recover from catastrophic strokes in 1965.

Flying

from *Roald Dahl*

by Jeremy Treglown

Dahl ... was too tall to fit comfortably into a cockpit (his inventive fellow trainees gave him his RAF nickname of Lofty) but he told his mother that, apart from that and the fact that he missed having servants, he had never enjoyed himself so much as during these weeks of flying Tiger Moths over the Kenyan Highlands. From there he moved to the bleaker surroundings of Habbaniya in the Iraqi desert, where he spent six months learning to shoot, to dive-bomb, to navigate and to fly at night before being passed on to a pilots' pool in Ismailia, Egypt. In mid-September 1940 his orders came through to join 80 Squadron in western Egypt, near the frontier with Libya.

Italy had formally entered the war in June, effectively closing the Mediterranean and cutting off much of the British land forces. Since then the Italians had been building up their strength in eastern Libya. The expected push into Egypt began on 13 September, when a large Italian army began a sixty-mile advance across the border, halting at Sidi Barrani on 18 September.

In all this, 80 Squadron had been kept busy and was forced frequently to move both its main headquarters and its landing grounds. The nineteenth of September was quiet: the squadron's officers organised a cricket match with the senior NCOs. Three hundred and fifty miles to their east Dahl took off from Abu Suweir in a Gloster Gladiator, a type of aeroplane he had not flown before. He stopped twice to refuel, the second time at Fuka, where he was given directions that may have been confused by events. His squadron was not where he expected to find it, and as dusk gathered over the North African desert and his fuel gauge fell, he decided to try to land.

Dahl described the crash in *Going Solo* as well as in 'Shot Down Over Libya' and its subsequent, less heroic version 'A Piece of Cake'. The squadron's own report the next day was typically low-key:

> Weather – wind N.W. – visibility good. A patrol was carried out over Mersa Matruh with 6 Gladiators from 1645 hours to 1800 hours. No enemy aircraft were sighted. P/O Dahl posted to this squadron from T.U.R.P. for flying duties w.e.f. 20th September. This pilot was ferrying an aircraft from No. 102 M.U. to this unit, but unfortunately not being used to flying aircraft over the Desert he made a forced landing 2 miles west of Mersa Matruh. He made an unsuccessful forced landing and the aircraft burst into flames. The pilot was badly burned and he was conveyed to an Army Field Ambulance Station.

It was seven months before anyone in 80 Squadron saw Dahl again. Anyone, that is, who lived that long.

On landing, the Gladiator had hit a boulder and lurched forward into the sand. In the collision Dahl's skull was fractured by hitting the metal reflector-sight and his nose was driven back into his face. Before the aircraft's petrol tanks caught fire he managed to extricate himself from his seat belt and parachute harness, crawl from the cockpit and roll out of danger, to be picked up, bleeding profusely, by British soldiers patrolling nearby.

The squadron report was wrong about his burns,

which were only slight, but his face was so swollen with bruises that he was blind for several weeks, and the injuries to his head, nose and back were such that it was almost two months before he was sufficiently recovered to get out of his hospital bed in Alexandria. On 20 November he wrote to his mother, from whom he had just received eight letters. With the bravado he always put on for her, he said that apart from persistent headaches he was feeling fine. The weather was like an English summer. He had been visited by some Norwegian expatriates and would be convalescing with wealthy local volunteers who took in wounded officers. Later, when his nose had been rebuilt, he was offered a berth home on the next convoy; he was afraid that it would mean no more flying, so he declined.

The decision took some courage. While he was in hospital Italy invaded Greece, which Britain, jointly with France, had before the war promised to defend. Since France had by now fallen, Britain could have argued that she was no longer bound by an agreement which, given the reversals of the North African campaign and the dangers of a German invasion at home, she couldn't have been worse placed to fulfil. The British Commander-in-Chief in the Middle East, General Wavell, warned Churchill that his forces were already over-stretched and that if they managed to secure an Italian withdrawal from Greece, the Germans would inevitably be drawn in through the Balkans. With the encouragement of US material aid, and buoyed up by what the historian John Terraine calls the 'strategic fantasies' of Churchill, the pro-Greek arguments prevailed. In November and December 1940, British aircraft badly needed in North Africa were sent to Greece; they included three squadrons of Blenheim bombers and two of Gladiator fighters – Squadrons 80 and 112.

As Terraine observes, 'From bad beginnings, things went from worse to worse.' Aircraft and spares were in short supply in Britain, let alone in the Middle East. Winter brought thick mists and low cloud to the mountains of Greece and earthquakes destroyed two airfields. The Greek High Command vacillated in its strategy and in the demands it made of its allies. As Wavell had predicted, Italian failures brought German reinforcements. By the time the British army's expeditionary force arrived on 5 March, its air support consisted of 200 aircraft (including reserves) against 800 German aircraft on the eastern front, 160 Italian in Albania and a further 150 based in Italy but within range of Greece. Two days earlier Churchill had told his Foreign Secretary, 'We do not see any reasons for expecting success.'

During this time, while Dahl was still in Alexandria, 80 Squadron took heavy losses both of pilots and aircraft. There were some triumphant days, including one at the beginning of March when members of the squadron – including its most famous pilot, Thomas Pattle, and the Commanding Officer, 'Tap' Jones – claimed over twenty Italian bombers and fighters shot down for no loss: a figure made much of in British and Greek propaganda. But Tap Jones himself, who ended up as an Air Marshal (and whom Dahl later falsely maligned as never having flown in combat), remembers it all as 'a most horrid campaign' in which the RAF were outnumbered, frustrated by bad weather and inadequate equipment, and were losing pilots sometimes at the rate of three or four a day.

On 6 April Germany invaded, and within ten days the 60,000 men of the British army in Greece were in full retreat. This was the situation when Dahl arrived from Egypt, flying another unfamiliar aeroplane: one of the much-needed Hurricanes with which 80 Squadron's Gladiators were being replaced. He would be in Greece for less than two weeks, but it was to be one of the most intense periods of his life, and certainly the most dangerous.

Autobiography

From its Greek origin the word *auto+bio+graphy* means self-life-writing – writing about one's own life. The critic R. Pascal said that people write autobiographies as 'a search for one's innerstanding' (*Design and Truth in Autobiography*). In other words, autobiographies can serve a similar purpose to diaries – helping us to shape the disorderly events of our lives and to come to a clearer sense of who we are. But this doesn't explain why we *read* autobiographies. Perhaps, as with biographies, it is our fascination with seeing beneath the public surface of people we admire, or simply want to know more about. Key features: a narrative structure (start with birth, end with old age); use of fictional techniques (characterisation, sense of people and place) to bring events to life; use of first-person mode (*I* rather than *she* or *he*) . . .

Survival

from *Going Solo*

by Roald Dahl

Some forty years ago I described in a story called 'A Piece of Cake' what it was like to find myself strapped firmly into the cockpit of my Gladiator with a fractured skull and a bashed-in face and a fuzzy mind while the crashed plane was going up in flames on the sands of the Western Desert. But there is an aspect of that story that I feel ought to be clarified by me and it is this. There seems, on rereading it, to be an implication that I was shot down by enemy action, and if I remember rightly, this was inserted by the editors of an American magazine called the *Saturday Evening Post* who originally bought and published it. Those were the war years and the more dramatic the story, the better it was. They actually called it 'Shot Down in Libya', so you can see what they were getting at. The fact is that my crash had nothing whatsoever to do with enemy action. I was not shot down either by another plane or from the ground. Here is what happened.

I had climbed into my new Gladiator at an RAF airfield called Abu Suweir on the Suez Canal, and had set off alone to join 80 Squadron in the Western Desert. This was going to be my very first venture into combat territory. The date was 19 September 1940. They told me to fly across the Nile delta and land at a small airfield called Amiriya, near Alexandria, to refuel. Then I should fly on and land again at a bomber airfield in Libya called Fouka for a second refuelling. At Fouka I was to report to the Commanding Officer who would tell me precisely where 80 Squadron were at that moment, and I would then fly on and join them. A forward airfield in the Western Desert was in those days never much more than a strip of sand surrounded by tents and parked aircraft, and these airfields were being moved very frequently from one site to another, depending on whether the front line of the army was advancing or retreating.

The flight in itself was a fairly daunting one for someone who had virtually no experience of the aircraft he was flying and none at all of flying long distances over Egypt and Libya with no navigational aids to help him. I had no radio. All I had was a map strapped to one knee. It took me one hour exactly to get from Abu Suweir to Amiriya where I landed with some difficulty in a sandstorm. But I got my plane refuelled and set off as quickly as I could for Fouka. I landed at Fouka fifty-five minutes later (all these times are meticulously recorded in my Log Book) and reported to the CO in his tent. He made some calls on his field telephone and then asked me for my map.

'Eighty Squadron are now there,' he said, pointing to a spot in the middle of the desert about thirty miles due south of the small coastal town of Mersah Matrûh.

'Will it be easy to see?' I asked him.

'You can't miss it,' he said. 'You'll see the tents and about fifteen Gladiators parked around the place. You can spot it from miles away.' I thanked him and went off to calculate my course and distance.

The time was 6.15 p.m. when I took off from Fouka for 80 Squadron's landing strip. I estimated my flight time to be fifty minutes at the most. That would give me fifteen or twenty minutes to spare before darkness fell, which should be ample.

I flew straight for the point where the 80 Squadron airfield should have been. It wasn't there. I flew around the area to north, south, east and west, but there was not a sign of an airfield. Below me there was nothing but empty desert, and rather rugged desert at that, full of large stones and boulders and gullies.

At this point, dusk began to fall and I realised that I was in trouble. My fuel was running low and there was no way I could get back to Fouka on what I had left. I couldn't have found it in the dark anyway. The only course open to me now was to make a forced landing in the desert and make it quickly, before it was too dark to see.

I skimmed low over the boulder-strewn desert searching for just one small strip of reasonably flat sand on which to land. I knew the direction of the wind so I knew precisely the direction that my approach should take. But where, oh where was there one little patch of desert that was clear of boulders and gullies and lumps of rock. There simply wasn't one. It was nearly dark now. I *had* to get down somehow or other. I chose a piece of ground that seemed to me to be as boulder-free as any and I made an approach. I came in as slowly as I dared, hanging on the prop, travelling just above my stalling speed of eighty miles an hour. My wheels touched down. I throttled back and prayed for a bit of luck.

I didn't get it. My undercarriage hit a boulder and collapsed completely and the Gladiator buried its nose in the sand at what must have been about seventy-five miles an hour.

My injuries in that bust-up came from my head being thrown forward violently against the reflector-sight when the plane hit the ground (in spite of the fact that I was strapped tightly, as always, into the cockpit), and apart from the skull fracture, the blow pushed my nose in and knocked out a few teeth and blinded me completely for days to come.

It is odd that I can remember very clearly quite a few of the things that followed seconds after the crash. Obviously I was unconscious for some moments, but I must have recovered my senses very quickly because I can remember hearing a mighty *whoosh* as the petrol tank in the port wing exploded, followed almost at once by another mighty *whoosh* as the starboard tank went up in flames. I could see nothing at all, and I felt no pain. All I wanted was to go gently off to sleep and to hell with the flames. But soon a tremendous heat around my legs galvanised my soggy brain into action. With great difficulty I managed to undo first my seat-straps and then the straps of my parachute, and I can even remember the desperate effort it took to push myself upright in the cockpit and roll out head first on to the sand below. Again I wanted to lie down and doze off, but the heat close by was terrific and had I stayed where I was I should simply have been roasted alive. I began very very slowly to drag myself away from the awful hotness. I heard my machine-gun ammunition exploding in the flames and the bullets were pinging about all over the place but that didn't worry me. All I wanted was to get away from the tremendous heat and rest in peace. The world about me was divided sharply down the middle into two halves. Both of these halves were pitch black, but one was scorching-hot and the other was not. I had to keep on dragging myself away from the scorching-hot side and into the cooler one, and this took a long time and enormous effort, but in the end the temperature all around me became bearable. When that happened I collapsed and went to sleep.

It was revealed at an inquiry into my crash held later that the CO at Fouka had given me totally wrong information. Eighty Squadron had never been in the position I was sent to. They were fifty miles to the south, and the place to which I had been sent was actually no-man's-land, which was a strip of sand in the Western Desert about half a mile wide dividing the front lines of the British and Italian armies. I am told that the flames from my burning aircraft lit up the sand dunes for miles around, and of course not only the crash but also the subsequent bonfire were witnessed by the soldiers of both sides. The watchers in the trenches had been observing my antics for some time, and both sides knew that it was an RAF fighter and not an Italian plane that had come down. The remains, if any, were therefore of more interest to our people than to the enemy.

When the flames had died down and the desert was dark, a little patrol of three brave men from the Suffolk Regiment crawled out from the British lines to inspect the wreck. They did not think for one moment that they would find anything but a burnt-out fuselage and a charred skeleton, and they were apparently astounded when they came upon my still-breathing body lying in the sand nearby.

When they turned me over in the dark to get a better look, I must have swum back into consciousness because I can distinctly remember hearing one of them asking me how I felt, but I was unable to reply. Then I heard them whispering together about how they were going to get me back to the lines without a stretcher.

The next thing I can remember a long time later was a man's voice speaking loudly to me and telling me that he knew I was unable to see him or to answer him, but he thought there was a chance I could hear him. He told me he was an English doctor and that I was in an underground first-aid post in Mersah Matrûh. He said they were going to take me to the train by ambulance and send me back to Alexandria.

I heard him talking to me and I understood what he was saying, and I also knew all about Mersah Matrûh and about the train. Mersah was a small town about 250 miles along the Libyan coast west of Alexandria, and our army had a most carefully preserved little railway running across the desert between the two places. This railway was a vital supply line for our forward troops in the Western Desert and the Italians were bombing it all the time but we somehow managed to keep it going. Everyone knew about the single-track railway-line that ran all the way along the coast beside the sparkling white beaches of the southern Mediterranean from Alex to Mersah.

I heard voices around me as they manoeuvred my stretcher into the ambulance, and when the ambulance started to move forward over the very bumpy track, someone above me began screaming. Every time we hit a bump the man above me cried out in agony.

When they were putting me on to the train, I felt a hand on my shoulder and a lovely Cockney voice said, 'Cheer up, matey. You'll soon be back in Alex.'

The next thing I can remember was being taken off the train into the tremendous bustle of Alexandria Station, and I heard a woman's voice saying, 'This one's an officer. He'll go to the Anglo-Swiss.'

Then I was inside the hospital itself and I heard the wheels of my stretcher rumbling softly along endless corridors. 'Put him in here for the moment,' a different woman's voice was saying. 'We want to have a look at him before he goes into the ward.'

Deft fingers began to unroll the bandages around my head. 'Can you hear me talking to you?' the owner of the fingers was saying. She took one of my hands in hers and said, 'If you can hear what I am saying, just give my hand a squeeze.' I squeezed her hand. 'Good,' she said. 'That's fine. Now we know you're going to be all right.'

Then she said, 'Here he is, doctor. I've taken off the dressings. He is conscious and is responding.'

I felt the close proximity of the doctor's face as he bent over me, and I heard him saying, 'Do you have much pain?'

Now that the bandages had been taken off my head, I found myself able to burble an answer to him. 'No,' I said. 'No pain. But I can't see.'

'Don't worry about that,' the doctor said. 'All you've got to do is to lie very still. Don't move. Do you want to empty your bladder?'

'Yes,' I said.

'We'll help you,' he said, 'but don't move. Don't try to do anything for yourself.'

I believe they inserted a catheter because I felt them doing something down there and it hurt a bit, but then the pressure on my bladder went away.

'Just a dry dressing for the moment, Sister,' the doctor said. 'We'll X-ray him in the morning.'

Then I was in a ward with a lot of other men who talked and joked a good deal among themselves. I lay there dozing and feeling no pain at all, and later on the air-raid sirens started wailing and the ack-ack guns began opening up on all sides and I heard a lot of bombs exploding not very far away. I knew it was night-time now because that was when the Italian bombers came over seven nights a week to raid our navy in Alexandria harbour. I felt very calm and dreamy lying there listening to the terrific commotion of bombs and ack-ack going on outside. It was as though I had earphones on and all the noise was coming to me over the wireless from miles and miles away.

I knew when the morning came because the whole ward began to bustle and breakfasts were served all round. Obviously I couldn't eat because my whole head was sheathed in bandages with only small holes left for breathing. I didn't want to eat anyway. I was always sleepy. One of my arms was strapped to a board because tubes were going into the arm, but the other, the right arm, was free and once I explored the bandages on my head with my fingers. Then the Sister was saying to me, 'We are moving your bed into another room where it is quieter and you can be by yourself.'

So they wheeled me out of the ward into a single room, and over the next one or two or three days, I don't know how many, I submitted in a semi-daze to various procedures such as X-rays and being taken several times to the operating theatre. One of my more vivid recollections is of a conversation that went on in the theatre itself between a doctor and me. I knew I was in the theatre because they always told me where they were taking me, and this time the doctor said to me, 'Well, young man, we are going to use a super brand-new anaesthetic on you today. It's just come out from England and it is given by injection.' I had had short talks with this particular doctor several times. He was an anaesthetist and had visited me in my room before each operation to put his stethoscope on my chest and back. All my life I have taken an intense and inquisitive interest in every form of medicine, and even in those young days I had begun to ask the doctors a lot of questions. This man, perhaps because I was blind, always took the trouble to treat me as an intelligent listener.

'What is it called?' I asked him.

'Sodium pentathol,' he answered.

'And you have never used it before?'

'I have never used it myself,' he said, 'but it has been a great success back home as a pre-anaesthetic. It is very quick and comfortable.'

I could sense that there were quite a few other people, men and women, padding silently around the operating theatre in their rubber boots and I could hear the tinkling of instruments lifted and put down, and the talk of soft voices. Both my senses of smell and of hearing had become very acute since my blindness, and I had developed an instinctive habit of translating sounds and scents into a coloured mental picture. I was picturing the operating theatre now, so white and sterile with the masked and green-gowned inmates going priestlike about their separate tasks, and I wondered where the surgeon was, the great man who was going to do all the cutting and the stitching.

I was about to have a major operation performed on my face, and the man who was doing it had been a famous Harley Street plastic surgeon before the war, but now he was a Surgeon-Commander in the navy. One of the nurses had told me about his Harley Street days that morning. 'You'll be all right with him,' she had said. 'He's a wonder-worker. And it's all free. A job like you're having would be costing you five hundred guineas in civvy street.'

'You mean this is the very first time you've ever used this anaesthetic?' I said to the anaesthetist.

This time he didn't answer me directly. 'You'll love it,' he said. 'You go out like a light. You don't even have any sensation of losing consciousness as you do with all the others. So here we go. You'll just feel a little prick on the back of your hand.'

I felt the needle going into a vein on the top of my left hand and I lay there waiting for the moment when I would 'go out like a light'.

I was quite unafraid. I have never been frightened by surgeons or of being given an anaesthetic, and to this day, after some sixteen major operations on numerous parts of my body, I still have complete faith in all, or let me say *nearly* all, those men of medicine.

I lay there waiting and waiting and absolutely nothing happened. My bandages had been taken off for the operation, but my eyes were still permanently closed by the swellings on my face. One doctor had told me it was quite possible that my eyes had not been damaged at all. I doubted that myself. It seemed to me that I had been permanently blinded, and as I lay there in my quiet black room where all sounds, however tiny, had suddenly become twice as loud, I had plenty of time to think about what total blindness would mean in the future. Curiously enough, it did not frighten me. It did not even depress me. In a world where war was all around me and where I had ridden in dangerous little aeroplanes that roared and zoomed and crashed and caught fire, blindness, not to mention life itself, was no longer too important. Survival was not something one struggled for any more. I was already beginning to realise that the only way to conduct oneself in a situation where bombs rained down and bullets whizzed past, was to accept the dangers and all the consequences as calmly as possible. Fretting and sweating about it all was not going to help.

The doctor had tried to comfort me by saying that when you have contusions and swellings as massive as mine, you have to wait at least until the swellings go down and the incrustations of blood around the eyelids have come away. 'Give yourself a chance,' he had said. 'Wait until those eyelids are able to open again.'

Having at this moment no eyelids to open and shut, I hoped the anaesthetist wouldn't start thinking that his famous new wonder anaesthetic had put me to sleep when it hadn't. I didn't want them to start before I was ready. 'I'm still awake,' I said.

'I know you are,' he said.

'What's going on?' I heard another man's voice asking. 'Isn't it working?' This, I knew, was the surgeon, the great man from Harley Street.

'It doesn't seem to be having any effect at all,' the anaesthetist said.

'Give him some more.'

'I have, I have,' the anaesthetist answered, and I thought I detected a slightly ruffled edge to the man's voice.

'London said it was the greatest discovery since chloroform,' the surgeon was saying. 'I saw the report myself. Matthews wrote it. Ten seconds, it said, and the patient's out. Simply tell him to count to ten and he's out before he gets to eight, that's what the report said.'

'This patient could have counted to a hundred,' the anaesthetist was saying.

It occurred to me that they were talking to one another as though I wasn't there. I would have been happier if they had kept quiet.

'Well, we can't wait all day,' the surgeon was saying. It was *his* turn to get irritable now. But I did not want my surgeon to be irritable when he was about to perform a delicate operation on my face. He had come into my room the day before and after examining me carefully, he had said, 'We can't have you going about like that for the rest of your life, can we?'

That worried me. It would have worried anyone. 'Like what?' I had asked him.

'I am going to give you a lovely new nose,' he had said, patting me on the shoulder. 'You want to have something nice to look at when you open your eyes again, don't you. Did you ever see Rudolph Valentino in the cinema?'

'Yes,' I said.

'I shall model your nose on his,' the surgeon said. 'What do you think of Rudolph Valentino, Sister?'

'He's smashing,' the Sister said.

And now, in the operating theatre, that same surgeon was saying to the anaesthetist, 'I'd forget that pentathol stuff if I were you. We really can't wait any longer. I've got four more on my list this morning.'

'Right!' snapped the anaesthetist. 'Bring me the nitrous oxide.'

I felt the rubber mask being put over my nose and mouth, and soon the blood-red circles began going round and round faster and faster like a series of gigantic scarlet flywheels and then there was an explosion and I knew nothing more.

When I regained consciousness I was back in my room. I lay there for an uncounted number of weeks but you must not think that I was totally without company during that time. Every morning throughout those black and sightless days a nurse, always the same one, would come into my room and bathe my eyes with something soft and wet. She was very gentle and very careful and she never hurt me. For at least an hour she would sit on my bed working skilfully on my swollen sealed-up eyes, and she would talk to me while she worked. She told me that the Anglo-Swiss used to be a large civilian hospital and that when war broke out the navy took over the whole place. All the doctors and all the nurses in the hospital were navy people, she said.

'Are you in the navy?' I asked her.

'Yes,' she said. 'I am a naval officer.'

'Why am *I* here if it's all navy?'

'We're taking in the RAF and the army as well now,' she said. 'That's where most of the casualties are coming from.'

Her name, she told me, was Mary Welland, and her home was in Plymouth. Her father was a Commander on a cruiser operating somewhere in the north Atlantic, and her mother worked with the Red Cross in Plymouth. She said with a smile in her voice that it was very bad form for a nurse to sit on a patient's bed, but what she was doing to my eyes was very delicate work that could only be done if she were sitting close to me. She had a lovely soft voice, and I began to picture to myself the face that went with the voice, the delicate features, the green-blue eyes, the golden-brown hair and the pale skin. Sometimes, as she worked very close to my eyes, I would feel her warm and faintly marmalade breath on my cheek and in no time at all I began to fall very quickly and quite dizzily in love with Mary Welland's invisible image. Every morning, I waited impatiently for the door to open and for the tinkling sound of the trolley as she wheeled it into my room.

Her features, I decided, were very much like those of Myrna Loy. Myrna Loy was a Hollywood cinema actress I had seen many times on the silver screen, and up until then she had been my idea of the perfect beauty. But now I took Miss Loy's face and made it even more beautiful and gave it to Mary Welland. The only concrete thing I had to go by was the voice, and so far as I was concerned, Mary Welland's dulcet tones were infinitely preferable to Myrna Loy's harsh American twang.

For about an hour every day I experienced ecstasy as Miss Myrna Mary Loy Welland sat on my bed and did things to my face and eyes with her delicate fingers. And then suddenly, I don't know how many days later, came the moment that I can never forget.

Mary Welland was working away on my right eye with one of her soft moist pads when all at once the eyelid began to open. At first it opened only an infinitesimal crack, but even so, a shaft of brilliant light pierced the darkness in my head and I saw before me very close ... I saw three separate things ... and all of them were glistening with scarlet and gold!

'I can see!' I cried. 'I can see something!'

'You can?' she said excitedly. 'Are you sure?'

'Yes! I can see something very close to me! I can see three separate things right in front of me! And nurse ... they are all shining with red and gold! What are they, nurse? What am I seeing?'

'Try to keep calm,' she said. 'Stop jumping up and down. It's not good for you.'

'But nurse, I really can see something! Don't you believe me?'

'Is this what you are seeing?' she asked me, and now part of a hand and a pointing finger came into my line of sight. 'Is it this? Is it these?' she said, and her finger pointed at the three beautiful things of many colours that lay there shimmering against a background of purest white.

'Yes!' I cried. 'It's those! There are three of them! I can see them all! And I can see your finger!'

When many days of blackness and doubt are pierced suddenly by shining images of red and gold, the pleasure that floods into your mind is overwhelming. I lay propped up on my pillows gazing through the tiny crack in one eye at these amazing sights and wondering whether I wasn't perhaps catching a glimpse of paradise. 'What am I looking at?' I asked her.

'You are looking at a bit of my white uniform,' Mary Welland said. 'It's the bit that goes across my front, and the coloured things you can see in the middle of it make up the emblem of the Royal Naval Nursing Service. It is pinned to the left side of my bosom and it is worn by all nurses in the Royal Navy.'

'But they are so *beautiful*!' I cried, staring at the emblem. There were three separate parts to it, all of them heavily embossed in raised embroidery. On top there was a golden crown with scarlet in the centre and small bits of green near its base. In the middle, below the crown, there was a gold anchor with a scarlet rope twined around it. And below the anchor there was a golden circle with a big red cross in the middle. These images and their brilliant colours have been engraved on my memory ever since.

'Keep still,' Mary Welland said. 'I think we can open this eyelid a bit more.'

I kept still and waited, and a few minutes later she succeeded in getting the eyelid wide open and I saw the whole room through that one eye. In the forefront of everything I saw Nursing Officer Welland herself sitting very close and smiling at me. 'Hello,' she said. 'Welcome back to the world.'

She was a lovely looking girl, much nicer than Myrna Loy and far more real. 'You are even more beautiful than I imagined,' I said.

'Well, thank you,' she said.

The next day she got the other eye open as well and I lay there feeling as though I was about to start my whole life over again.

Reportage

Matthew Arnold said 'Journalism is literature in a hurry'. We are used to getting news from television, radio and newspapers. But *we* all have news to give all the time: we are all eyewitnesses, even if the events themselves don't seem significant. This section shows people acting as eyewitnesses and reporting what they see – Elizabeth Bentley reporting on factory conditions for children; Charles Dickens re-creating the conditions of his own factory experiences. Key ingredients: a sense of interest or fascination in what is being observed, an intention to communicate it to others, a straightforward, informative style, attention to detail of people and place . . .

Factory Conditions in 1815

from the *Report of the Parliamentary Committee to Regulate the Labour of Children*

by Elizabeth Bentley

What age are you?
   Twenty-three.

Where do you live?
   At Leeds.

What time did you begin work at the factory?
   When I was six years old.

At whose factory did you work?
   Mr Burk's.

What kind of mill is it?
   Flax mill.

What was your business in that mill?
   I was a little doffer.

What were your hours of labour in that mill?
   From 5 in the morning till 9 at night, when they were thronged.

For how long a time together have you worked that excessive length of time?
   For about a year.

What were the usual hours of labour when you were not so thronged?
   From six in the morning till 7 at night.

What time was allowed for meals?
Forty minutes at noon.

Had you any time to get your breakfast or drinking?
No, we had to get it as we could.

Do you consider doffing a laborious employment?
Yes.

Explain what you had to do.
When the frames are full, they have to stop the frames, and take the flyers off, and take the full bobbins off, and carry them to the roller, and then put empty ones on, and set the frame going again.

Does that keep you constantly on your feet?
Yes, there are so many frames and they run so quick.

Your labour is very excessive?
Yes, you have not time for anything.

Suppose you flagged a little, or were late, what would they do?
Strap us.

And they are in the habit of strapping those who are last in doffing?
Yes.

Constantly?
Yes.

Girls as well as boys?
Yes.

Have you ever been strapped?
Yes.

Severely?
Yes.

Is the strap used so as to hurt you excessively?

Yes it is ... I have seen the overlooker go to the top end of the room, where the little girls hug the can to the backminders; he has taken a strap, and a whistle in his mouth, and sometimes he has got a chain and chained them, and strapped them all down the room.

What was his reason for that?

He was very angry.

Did you live far from the mill?

Yes, two miles.

Had you a clock?

No, we had not.

Were you generally there in time?

Yes, my mother has been up at 4 o'clock in the morning, and at 2 o'clock in the morning; the colliers used to go to their work at 3 or 4 o'clock, and when she heard them stirring she has got up out of her warm bed, and gone out and asked them the time; and I have sometimes been at Hunslet Car at 2 o'clock in the morning, when it was streaming down with rain, and we have had to stay till the mill was opened.

You are considerably deformed in person as a consequence of this labour?

Yes I am.

And what time did it come on?

I was about 13 years old when it began coming, and it has got worse since; it is five years since my mother died, and my mother was never able to get me a good pair of stays to hold me up, and when my mother died I had to do for myself, and got me a pair.

Were you perfectly straight and healthy before you worked at a mill?

Yes, I was as straight a little girl as ever went up and down town.

Were you straight till you were 13?

Yes, I was.

Did your deformity come upon you with much pain and weariness?

Yes, I cannot express the pain all the time it was coming.

Do you know of anybody that has been similarly injured in their health?

Yes, in their health, but not many deformed as I am.

It is very common to have weak ankles and crooked knees?

Yes, very common indeed.

This is brought on by stopping the spindle?

Yes.

Where are you now?

In the poorhouse.

State what you think as to the circumstances in which you have been placed during all this time of labour, and what you have considered about it as to the hardship and cruelty of it.

The witness was too much affected to answer the question.

Dickens Recalls the Blacking Warehouse

from *The Life of Charles Dickens*

by John Forster

The blacking warehouse was the last house on the left-hand side of the way, at old Hungerford-stairs. It was a crazy, tumble-down old house, abutting of course on the river, and literally overrun with rats. Its wainscotted rooms, and its rotten floors and staircase, and the old grey rats swarming down in the cellars, and the sound of their squeaking and scuffling coming up the stairs at all times, and the dirt and decay of the place, rise up visibly before me, as if I were there again. The counting-house was on the first floor, looking over the coal-barges and the river. There was a recess in it, in which I was to sit and work. My work was to cover the pots of paste-blacking; first with a piece of oil-paper, and then with a piece of blue paper; to tie them round with a string; and then to clip the paper close and neat, all round, until it looked as smart as a pot of ointment from an apothecary's shop. When a certain number of grosses of pots had attained this pitch of perfection, I was to paste on each a printed label; and then go on again with more pots. Two or three other boys were kept at similar duty down stairs on similar wages. One of them came up, in a ragged apron and a paper cap, on the first Monday morning, to show me the trick of using the string and tying the knot. His name was Bob Fagin; and I took the liberty of using his name, long afterwards, in *Oliver Twist*. . . .

No words can express the secret agony of my soul as I sunk into this companionship; compared these every-day associates with those of my happier childhood; and felt my early hopes of growing up to be a learned and distinguished man, crushed in my breast. The deep remembrance of the sense I had of being utterly neglected and hopeless; of the shame I felt in my position; of the misery it was to my young heart to believe that, day by day, what I had learned, and thought, and delighted in, and raised my fancy and my emulation up by, was passing away from me, never to be brought back any more; cannot be written....

I was such a little fellow, with my poor white hat, little jacket, and corduroy trowsers, that frequently, when I went into the bar of a strange public-house for a glass of ale or porter to wash down the saveloy and the loaf I had eaten in the street, they didn't like to give it me. I remember, one evening (I had been somewhere for my father, and was going back to the borough over Westminster-bridge), that I went into a public-house in Parliament-street, which is still there though altered, at the corner of the short street leading into Cannon-row, and said to the landlord behind the bar, 'What is your best – the VERY *best* – ale, a glass?' For, the occasion was a festive one, for some reason: I forget why. It may have been my birthday, or somebody else's. 'Two-pence,' says he. 'Then,' says I, 'just draw me a glass of that, if you please, with a good head to it.' The landlord looked at me, in return, over the bar, from head to foot, with a strange smile on his face; and instead of drawing the beer, looked round the screen and said something to his wife, who came out from behind it, with her work in her hand, and joined him in surveying me. Here we stand, all three, before me now, in my study in

Devonshire-terrace. The landlord, in his shirt sleeves, leaning against the bar window-frame; his wife, looking over the little half-door; and I, in some confusion, looking up at them from outside the partition. They asked me a good many questions, as what my name was, how old I was, where I lived, how I was employed, etc. etc. To all of which, that I might commit nobody, I invented appropriate answers. They served me with the ale, though I suspect it was not the strongest on the premises; and the landlord's wife, opening the little half-door and bending down, gave me a kiss that was half-admiring and half-compassionate, but all womanly and good, I am sure.

Diaries

Writer Ronald Blythe said that 'The first diarists wrote to bring some kind of systematising to the rich muddle of their lives.' We all feel sometimes that our lives are muddled and spiralling out of control. For some people, diaries give them the chance to sort out the events of the day, to reflect on what has happened. While major events might be recorded in diaries, unlike reportage their audience is private: most diaries are written for the writer and no one else. Key ingredients: attention to details of events, people and places; a reflective, strongly personal tone; a sense of writing purely for oneself; a first-person narrative style (*I* rather than *she* or *he*) . . .

Nothing Could Be Crueller

Lady Cynthia Asquith

Saturday, 1 July 1916

I don't know how to write about this awful day. I didn't
expect Beb till 2.20, so had arranged to lunch with my
grandmother. Was back soon after two, ran into room
in high spirits. Beb said, 'I'm afraid there's bad news',
and gave me an opened letter from Papa. 'The worst is
true about Ego. The officer prisoners of Angora certify
that he was killed at Katia ... I have wired to Guy
Wyndham at Clouds. I don't know how Letty will be
told. It is very cruel and we must all help each other to
bear it.'

Oh God – Oh God, my beautiful brother that I have
loved so since I was a baby – so beautiful *through* and
through! Can it be true that he'll never come back? At
first I could only think of Letty, just the blank horror of
that gripped me. Mamma's away at Clouds – that's
unthinkable, too! Letty will occupy her for the first
days, but afterwards I'm so frightened for her.

Papa telephoned to me and I went round to Cadogan
Square. Poor, poor Papa! He really proudly loved those
two perfect sons. He said he had been round to Kakoo
– she expected John back in the afternoon and they
thought he had better tell Letty. Her mother was not
coming back till nine and Diana was away. We walked
round to Eaton Square together and found Kakoo in.
No John, and we discussed what had better be done.

Came to conclusion that if John had not arrived by five, Papa and I would go round to Letty. We telephoned and found out she would be in between five and six. I went home to Beb and waited – no message came, so after five I went to Cadogan Square and picked up poor Papa. The poignancy of what followed was so inconceivably beyond anything in my experience that I don't feel as if I could ever be unhaunted by it for a minute.

Letty was alone with the children playing the piano to them. Papa went up – I waited downstairs. The music stopped and I heard a gay 'Hulloa', then silence. I rushed up and found Letty clinging to Papa. It's indescribable – it was just like somebody in a fearful, unimaginable, physical pain. Streams of beautiful, eloquent words were torn from her heart. The children were scared. 'What has happened to you, Mummie? What is the matter with you? Will you be better in the morning?' I ran up to Sparks – she came and fetched them, and brought sal volatile and was wonderfully nice and good with Letty. We tried to make Letty go upstairs, but she wanted to stay down a little.

Papa was wonderfully sweet, and she seemed to cling to him: 'Oh Papa, it can't be true! How could God be so cruel? There was no one else in the world in the least like him – no one – I have been so wonderfully happy. His beautiful face, his smile … my Ego, come back to me. Oh God! Oh God! It's no use calling to God – nothing is any use – nothing in all the world can help him. I'm only twenty-eight – I'm so strong – I shan't die!'

Marjorie came in, perfectly self-controlled and bracing – spoke to Letty as you would to a housemaid being vaccinated. 'Now, now Letty – come, come.' At last we got her to go upstairs and carried her to her room. Then she saw his photographs and the bed. She sent for the children – his lovely little boys, and tried to make them understand. 'David, I want you to understand Poppa's – you remember what he looked like – Poppa's never coming back to us.' David said at once, 'But, I want him to ...' but he didn't understand and said, 'I must go now, or I shall be late for bed.' She was afraid that they would never remember him and the children – the one platitude one clung to for her – became one of the most poignant stabs.

Papa went away and I stayed alone with her. She got quieter. John came after six and took the line that there *was* hope with her, clinging to the fact that it was not 'official'. I have *none*. Is it cruel or kind to give it to her? I think one ought to give her the evidence, but not colour it with subjective optimism at all – she is so open to suggestion. Nothing could be crueller than the way it has come.

Amid the Blitz

Edward R. Murrow

8 September 1940

Yesterday afternoon – it seems days ago now – I drove
down to the East End of London, the East India Dock
Road, Commercial Road, through Silvertown, down to
the mouth of the Thames Estuary. It was a quiet and
almost pleasant trip through those streets running
between rows of working-class houses, with the cranes,
the docks, the ships, and the oil tanks off on the right.
We crossed the river and drove up on a little plateau,
which gave us a view from the mouth of the Thames to
London. And then an air-raid siren, called 'Weeping
Willie' by the men who tend it, began its uneven
screaming. Down on the coast the white puffballs of
anti-aircraft fire began to appear against a steel-blue
sky. The first flight of German bombers was coming up
the river to start the twelve-hour attack against London.
They were high and not very numerous. The Hurricanes and Spitfires were already in the air, climbing for
altitude above the nearby aerodrome. The fight moved
inland and out of sight. Things were relatively quiet for
about half an hour. Then the British fighters returned.
And five minutes later the German bombers, flying in
V-formation, began pouring in. The anti-aircraft fire
was good. Sometimes it seemed to burst right on the
nose of the leading machine, but still they came on. On
the aerodrome, ground crews swarmed over those

British fighters, fitting ammunition belts and pouring in petrol. As soon as one fighter was ready, it took the air, and there was no waiting for flight leaders or formation. The Germans were already coming back, down the river, heading for France.

Up toward London we could see billows of smoke fanning out above the river; and over our heads the British fighters, climbing almost straight up, trying to intercept the bombers before they got away. It went on for two hours and then the 'all-clear'. We went down to a nearby pub for dinner. Children were already organising a hunt for bits of shrapnel. Under some bushes beside the road there was a baker's cart. Two boys, still sobbing, were trying to get a quivering bay mare back between the shafts. The lady who ran the pub told us that these raids were bad for the chickens, the dogs, and the horses. A toothless old man of nearly seventy came in and asked for a pint of mild and bitter, confided that he had always, all his life, gone to bed at eight o'clock and found now that three pints of beer made him drowsy-like so he could sleep through any air raid.

Before eight the siren sounded again. We went back to a haystack near the aerodrome. The fires up river had turned the moon blood red. The smoke had drifted down till it formed a canopy over the Thames; the guns were working all round us, the bursts looking like fireflies in a southern summer night. The Germans were sending in two or three planes at a time, sometimes only one, in relays. They would pass overhead. The guns and lights would follow them, and in about five minutes we could hear the hollow grunt of the bombs. Huge pear-shaped bursts of flame would rise up into the smoke and disappear. The world was upside down. Vincent Sheean lay on one side of me and cursed in five languages; he'd talk about the war in Spain. Ben Robertson, of PM, lay on the other side and kept saying over and over in his slow South Carolina drawl, 'London is burning, London is burning.'

It was like a shuttle service, the way the German planes came up the Thames, the fires acting as a flare path. Often they were above the smoke. The search-lights bored into that black roof, but couldn't penetrate it. They looked like long pillars supporting a black canopy. Suddenly all the lights dashed off and black-ness fell right to the ground. It grew cold. We covered ourselves with hay. The shrapnel clicked as it hit the concrete road near by, and still the German bombers came.

Early this morning we went to a hotel. The gunfire rattled the windows. Shortly before noon we rang for coffee. A pale, red-eyed chambermaid brought it and said, 'I hope you slept well, sirs.' This afternoon we drove back to the East End of London. It was like an obstacle race – two blocks to the right, then left for four blocks, then straight on for a few blocks, and right again … streets roped off, houses and shops smashed … a few dirty-faced, tow-headed children standing on a corner, holding their thumbs up, the sign of the men who came back from Dunkirk … three red buses drawn up in a line waiting to take the homeless away … men with white scarfs round their necks instead of collars and ties, leading dull-eyed, empty-faced women across to the buses. Most of them carried little cheap cardboard suitcases and sometimes bulging paper shopping-bags. That was all they had left. There was still fire and smoke along the river, but the fire-fighters and the demolition squads have done their work well.

9 September 1940

I've spent the day visiting the bombed areas. The King did the same thing. These people may have been putting on a bold front for the King, but I saw them just as they were – men shovelling mounds of broken glass into trucks, hundreds of people being evacuated from the East End, all of them calm and quiet. In one street where eight or ten houses had been smashed a policeman stopped a motorist who had driven through a red light. The policeman's patience was obviously exhausted. As he made out his report and lectured the driver, everyone in the street gathered round to listen, paying no attention at all to the damaged houses; they were much more interested in the policeman.

These people are exceedingly brave, tough and prudent. The East End, where disaster is always just round the corner, seems to take it better than the more fashionable districts in the West End.

The firemen have done magnificent work these last forty-eight hours. Early this morning I watched them fighting a fire that was obviously being used as a beacon by the German bombers. The bombs came down only a few blocks away, but the firemen just kept their hoses playing steadily at the base of the flame.

The Germans dropped some very big stuff last night. One bomb, which fell about a quarter of a mile from where I was standing on a roof-top, made the largest crater I've ever seen, and I thought I'd seen some big ones. The blast travelled down nearby streets, smashing windows five or six blocks away.

The British shot down three of the night-bombers last night. I said a moment ago that Londoners were both brave and prudent. Tonight many theatres are closed. The managers decided that the crowds just wouldn't come. Tonight the queues were outside the air-raid shelters, not the theatres. In my district, people carrying blankets and mattresses began going to the shelters before the siren sounded.

This night bombing is serious and sensational.

Letters

Felix Pryor said: 'Most letters are very boring. It is perhaps for this reason that, contrary to popular belief, more are being written today than at any other time in history.' Letters can serve many purposes, but perhaps their key feature among written texts is that they are usually aimed at one person. As readers of other people's letters, therefore, we have an odd role – gazing into other people's lives and relationships. This section highlights some of the different purposes of letters . . .

My Unhappy Brother

Charlotte Brontë (to W. S. Williams)

2 October 1848

My dear Sir,

'We have buried our dead out of sight.' A lull begins to succeed the gloomy tumult of last week. It is not permitted us to grieve for him who is gone as others grieve for those they lose. The removal of our only brother must necessarily be regarded by us rather in the light of a mercy than a chastisement. Branwell was his father's and his sisters' pride and hope in boyhood, but since manhood the case has been otherwise. It has been our lot to see him take a wrong bent; to hope, expect, wait his return to the right path; to know the sickness of hope deferred, the dismay of prayer baffled; to experience despair at last – and now to behold the sudden early obscure close of what might have been a noble career.

I do not weep from a sense of bereavement – there is no prop withdrawn, no consolation torn away, no dear companion lost – but for the wreck of talent, the ruin of promise, the untimely dreary extinction of what might have been a burning and a shining light. My brother was a year my junior. I had aspirations and ambitions for him once, long ago – they have perished mournfully. Nothing remains of him but a memory of errors and sufferings. There is such a bitterness of pity for his life and death, such a yearning for the emptiness of his whole existence as I cannot describe. I trust time will allay these feelings.

My poor father naturally thought more of his *only* son than of his daughters, and, much and long as he had suffered on his account, he cried out of his loss like David for that of Absalom – my son! my son! – and refused at first to be comforted. And then when I ought to have been able to collect my strength and be at hand to support him, I fell ill with an illness whose approaches I had felt for some time previously, and of which the crisis was hastened by the awe and trouble of the death-scene – the first I had ever witnessed. The past has seemed to me a strange week. Thank God, for my father's sake, I am better now, though still feeble. I wish indeed I had more general physical strength – the want of it is sadly in my way. I cannot do what I would do for want of sustained animal spirits and efficient bodily vigour.

My unhappy brother never knew what his sisters had done in literature – he was not aware that they had ever published a line. We could not tell him of our efforts for fear of causing him too deep a pang of remorse for his own time misspent, and talents misapplied. Now he will *never* know. I cannot dwell longer on the subject at present – it is too painful.

I thank you for your kind sympathy, and pray earnestly that your sons may all do well, and that you may be spared the sufferings my father has gone through. – Yours sincerely,

C. BRONTË

Letter from No-Man's-Land

Wilfred Owen (to Susan Owen)

Tues: 16 January 1917   [*2nd Manchester Regt., B.E.F.*]

My own sweet Mother,

I am sorry you have had about 5 days letterless. I hope you had my two letters 'posted' since you wrote your last, which I received tonight. I am bitterly disappointed that I never got one of yours.

I can see no excuse for deceiving you about these last 4 days. I have suffered seventh hell.

I have not been at the front.

I have been in front of it.

I held an advanced post, that is, a 'dug-out' in the middle of No Man's Land.

We had a march of 3 miles over shelled road then nearly 3 along a flooded trench. After that we came to where the trenches had been blown flat out and had to go over the top. It was of course dark, too dark, and the ground was not mud, not sloppy mud, but an octopus of sucking clay, 3, 4, and 5 feet deep, relieved only by craters full of water. Men have been known to drown in them. Many stuck in the mud & only got on by leaving their waders, equipment, and in some cases their clothes.

High explosives were dropping all around out, and machine-guns spluttered every few minutes. But it was so dark that even the German flares did not reveal us.

Three-quarters dead, I mean each of us 3/4 dead, we reached the dug-out, and relieved the wretches therein. I then had to go forth and find another dug-out for a still more advanced post where I left 18 bombers. I was responsible for other posts on the left but there was a junior officer in charge.

My dug-out held 25 men tight packed. Water filled it to a depth of 1 or 2 feet, leaving say 4 feet of air.

One entrance had been blown in & blocked.

So far, the other remained.

The Germans knew we were staying there and decided we shouldn't.

Those fifty hours were the agony of my happy life.

Every ten minutes on Sunday afternoon seemed an hour.

I nearly broke down and let myself drown in the water that was now slowly rising over my knees.

Towards 6 o'clock, when, I suppose, you would be going to church, the shelling grew less intense and less accurate: so that I was mercifully helped to do my duty and crawl, wade, climb and flounder over No Man's Land to visit my other post. It took me half an hour to move about 150 yards.

I was chiefly annoyed by our own machine-guns from behind. The seeng-seeng-seeng of the bullets reminded me of Mary's canary. On the whole I can support the canary better.

In the Platoon on my left the sentries over the dug-out were blown to nothing. One of these poor fellows was my first servant whom I rejected. If I had kept him he would have lived, for servants don't do Sentry Duty. I kept my own sentries half-way down the stairs during the more terrific bombardment. In spite of this one lad was blown down and, I am afraid, blinded.

This was my only casualty.

The officer of the left Platoon has come out completely prostrated and is in hospital.

I am now as well, I suppose, as ever.

I allow myself to tell you all these things because <u>I am never going back to this awful post</u>. It is the worst the Manchesters have ever held; and we are going back for a rest.

I hear that the officer who relieved me left his 3 Lewis Guns behind when he came out. (He had only 24 hours in.) He will be court-martialled.

In conclusion, I must say that if there is any power whom the Soldiery execrate more than another it is that of our distinguished countryman.[1] You may pass it on via Owen, Owen.

Don't pass round these sheets but have portions typed for Leslie etc. My previous letter to you has just been returned. It will be too heavy to include in this.

Your very own
WILFRED X

[1] the Prime Minister, David Lloyd George

All this Madness

Bertrand Russell (to the *Nation*)

15 August 1914

Sir,

Against the vast majority of my countrymen, even at this moment, in the name of humanity and civilisation, I protest against our share in the destruction of Germany.

A month ago Europe was a peaceful comity of nations; if an Englishman killed a German he was hanged. Now, if an Englishman kills a German, or if a German kills an Englishman, he is a patriot, who has deserved well of his country. We scan the newspapers with greedy eyes for news of slaughter, and rejoice when we read of innocent young men, blindly obedient to the word of command, mown down in thousands by the machine-guns of Liège. Those who saw the London crowds during the nights leading up to the Declaration of War saw a whole population, hitherto peaceable and humane, precipitated in a few days down the steep slope of primitive barbarism, letting loose, in a moment, the instincts of hatred and blood lust against which the whole fabric of society has been raised. 'Patriots' in all countries acclaim this brutal orgy as a noble determination to vindicate the right; reason and mercy are swept away in one great flood of hatred; dim abstractions of unimaginable wickedness – Germany to us and the French, Russia to the Germans – conceal the simple fact that the enemy are men, like ourselves, neither better nor worse – men who love their homes and the sunshine, and all the simple pleasures of common lives; men now mad with terror in the thought of their wives, their sisters, their children, exposed, with our help, to the tender mercies of the conquering Cossack.

And all this madness, all this rage, all this flaming death of our civilisation and our hopes, has been brought about because a set of official gentlemen, living luxurious lives, mostly stupid, and all without imagination or heart, have chosen that it should occur rather than that any one of them should suffer some infinitesimal rebuff to his country's pride. . . .

And behind the diplomatists, dimly heard in the official documents, stand vast forces of national greed and national hatred – atavistic instincts, harmful to mankind at its present level, but transmitted from savage and half-animal ancestors, concentrated and directed by Governments and the Press, fostered by the upper class as a distraction from social discontent, artificially nourished by the sinister influence of the makers of armaments, encouraged by a whole foul literature of 'glory', and by every text-book of history with which the minds of children are polluted.

A Case of Sudden Death

Tracey Cramton (to *Practical Fishkeeping*)

Q I am writing to see if you can help with the unexplained death of my female Oranda.

We had her a few weeks and she seemed healthy, lively and fed well. She laid eggs a week or two ago. On Friday morning she was fine but that evening she looked 'hassled'; her fin was down, but not enough to cause us alarm. As the night progressed she began to hide in the corner, as if she was standing on her head with her tail in the air. She had never done this before. Early the next morning my husband found her dead. There are two other Orandas in the tank, both of which are fine.

• Tracey Cramton, Co. Durham

A It is very sad and disconcerting when a fish apparently in good health dies suddenly and for no obvious reason. Unfortunately, fish, like humans, are subject to sudden heart attacks. About two years ago I had a most unusual experience at a goldfish show when one of the exhibitors, to his dismay found one of his fish floating apparently lifeless in its bucket.

One of the bystanders suggested that the fish in the bucket was given a vigorous shaking in the water and lo and behold the fish's gill covers began to move and the fish gradually recovered not only to win its class but the Best in Show. Clearly what had happened was that the stress experienced by the fish had caused a cardiac arrest, subsequent treatment (equivalent to a heart massage) restarted the heart and the fish recovered.

From what you say about your fish, I suspect there was a heart problem, possibly from some organic cause which made itself felt on the Friday evening with subsequent death. It could have been something like an aneurysm in the blood circulatory system, but a post mortem would have to have been carried out to establish this.

JS

Speeches

Speech-writer Peggy Noonan (who wrote speeches for US President Ronald Reagan) described the power of speeches like this:

> A speech reminds us that words, like children, have the power to make dance the dullest beanbag of a heart ... They count. They more than count, they shape what happens. (*What I Saw at the Revolution*)

Where letters connect two people who usually know each other, a speech connects one person with possibly thousands. Its key features, therefore, are usually important themes, clear, often repetitive sentence patterns, use of emotive language (words like *freedom, power, trust* and *truth*), use of first- and second-person narrative forms (*I* but also *you, we* and *us*) and a rousing conclusion ...

How Can You Buy or Sell the Sky?

Chief Seattle (to the President of the United States, 1854)

How can you buy or sell the sky, the warmth of the land? The idea is strange to us.

If we do not own the freshness of the air and the sparkle of the water, how can you buy them?

Every part of this earth is sacred to my people.

Every shining pine needle, every sandy shore, every mist in the dark woods, every clearing and humming insect is holy in the memory and experience of my people. The sap which courses through the trees carried the memories of the red man.

The white man's dead forget the country of their birth when they go to walk among the stars. Our dead never forget this beautiful earth, for it is the mother of the red man.

We are part of the earth and it is part of us. The perfumed flowers are our sisters; the deer, the horse, the great eagle, these are our brothers.

The rocky crests, the juices in the meadows, the body heat of the pony, and man – all belong to the same family.

So, when the Great Chief in Washington sends word that he wishes to buy our land, he asks much of us. The Great Chief sends word he will reserve us a place so that we can live comfortably to ourselves.

He will be our father and we will be his children. So we will consider your offer to buy our land.

But it will not be easy. For this land is sacred to us.

This shining water that moves in the streams and rivers is not just water but the blood of our ancestors.

If we sell you land, you must remember that it is sacred, and you must teach your children that it is sacred and that each ghostly reflection in the clear water of the lakes tells of events and memories in the life of my people.

The water's murmur is the voice of my father's father.

The rivers are our brothers, they quench our thirst. The rivers carry our canoes, and feed our children. If we sell you our land, you must remember, and teach your children, that the rivers are our brothers, and yours, and you must henceforth give the rivers the kindness you would give any brother.

We know that the white man does not understand our ways. One portion of land is the same to him as the next, for he is a stranger who comes in the night and takes from the land whatever he needs.

The earth is not his brother, but his enemy, and when he has conquered it, he moves on.

He leaves his father's graves behind, and he does not care. He kidnaps the earth from his children, and he does not care.

His father's grave and his children's birthright, are forgotten. He treats his mother, the earth, and his brother, the sky, as things to be bought, plundered, sold like sheep or bright beads.

His appetite will devour the earth and leave behind only a desert.

I do not know. Our ways are different from your ways.

The sight of your cities pains the eyes of the red man. But perhaps it is because the red man is a savage and does not understand.

There is no quiet place in the white man's cities. No

place to hear the unfurling of leaves in spring, or the rustle of an insect's wings.

But perhaps it is because I am a savage and do not understand.

The clatter only seems to insult the ears. And what is there to life if a man cannot hear the lonely cry of the whippoorwill or the arguments of the frogs around a pond at night? I am a red man and do not understand.

The Indian prefers the soft sound of the wind darting over the face of a pond, and the smell of the wind itself, cleaned by a midday rain, or scented with the pinon pine.

The air is precious to the red man, for all things share the same breath – the beast, the tree, the man, they all share the same breath.

The white man does not seem to notice the air he breathes. Like a man dying for many days, he is numb to the stench.

But if we sell you our land, you must remember that the air is precious to us, that the air shares its spirit with all the life it supports. The wind that gave our grandfather his first breath also receives his last sigh.

And if we sell you our land, you must keep it apart and sacred, as a place where even the white man can go to taste the wind that is sweetened by the meadow's flowers.

So we will consider your offer to buy our land. If we decide to accept, I will make one condition: the white man must treat the beasts of this land as his brother.

I am a savage and I do not understand any other way.

I have seen a thousand rotting buffaloes on the prairie, left by the white man who shot them from a passing train.

I am a savage and I do not understand how the

smoking iron horse can be more important than the buffalo that we kill only to stay alive.

What is man without the beasts? If all the beasts were gone, man would die from a great loneliness of spirit.

For whatever happens to the beasts, soon happens to man. All things are connected.

You must teach your children that the ground beneath their feet is the ashes of your grandfathers. So that they will respect the land, tell your children that the earth is rich with the lives of our kin.

Teach your children what we have taught our children, that the earth is our mother.

Whatever befalls the earth befalls the sons of the earth. If men spit upon the ground, they spit upon themselves.

This we know: the earth does not belong to man; man belongs to the earth. This we know.

All things are connected like the blood which unites one family. All things are connected.

Whatever befalls the earth befalls the sons of the earth. Man did not weave the web of life: he is merely a strand in it. Whatever he does to the web, he does to himself.

Even the white man, whose God walks and talks with him as friend to friend, cannot be exempt from the common destiny.

We may be brothers after all.

We shall see.

One thing we know, which the white man may one day discover – our God is the same God.

You may think now that you own Him as you wish to own our land; but you cannot. He is the God of man, and His compassion is equal for the red man and the white.

This earth is precious to Him, and to harm the earth is to heap contempt on its Creator.

The whites too shall pass; perhaps sooner than all other tribes. Contaminate your bed, and you will one night suffocate in your own waste.

But in your perishing you will shine brightly, fired by the strength of the God who brought you to this land and for some special purpose gave you dominion over this land and over the red man.

That destiny is a mystery to us, for we do not understand when the buffalo are all slaughtered, the wild horses are tamed, the secret corners of the forest heavy with scent of many men, and the view of the ripe hills blotted by talking wires.

Where is the thicket? Gone.

Where is the eagle? Gone.

The end of living and the beginning of survival.

We Women Are the Weaker Sex

Emmeline Pankhurst (to the WSPU, London, 30 November 1914)

We women are the weaker sex. (*Laughter.*) We have been told that our hands are full with our domestic concerns and our maternal duties. In times of peace we have a good deal to say on that, but in times of war we are compelled to take men at their word. Men say to us, 'Leave the fighting to us. It does not become women to fight. We protect women. We fight for you. We shield you from the difficulties and ills of life.' Well, this is a testing time for men and women, too. We take you, gentlemen, at your word. We say it is the duty of men to do their best to redeem their pledges to women. We have not been allowed to prepare ourselves for self-defence because we are women. ('*Hear, hear*' ...)

During the last few days I have been thanking God I was not a superior person (*laughter*), and that I had not a facile pen or a great sense of saturnine humour so that I must indulge in something parallel to Nero's fiddling while Rome burned. I cannot find words strong enough to condemn the people who at this moment are haggling with imperfect knowledge over diplomacy and what led to the war, and who is to blame for it. I will tell you who is to blame if things are not as they ought to be. It is you enfranchised men. It is the Bernard Shaws and all the rest of them. (*Cheers and laughter.*) They say the science of government is only suited to the male sex. Then when you face a great national peril and your very existence as a nation is at stake, they begin to argue in newspaper columns in order that our enemy may quote them on the walls of Belgium. If we have rulers who are wrongdoers, it is the fault of the people who made them rulers. When the war is over will be the time to settle these questions of diplomacy. Here we are in the war. Our honour, our reputation, our very existence are at stake. It is a time for people either to criticise helpfully or to hold their tongues. If we women, with our grievances against men, can hold our tongues, I think other people might do so. (*Cheers.*) If there are mistakes, the right and proper thing to do if you love your country is to try to get things put right quietly by influence . . . .

The views I have always held I still hold. Nothing is more horrible than wars of aggression. But I believe that, whatever faults we have had in the past, now we are engaged in a righteous war. Much as I love peace, I believe there are times when it is right to fight. And I say to young men: There are women today who never thought to envy men their manhood, but who would, at least for this purpose, be glad to be men. (*Cheers.*)

Technical writing

Technical and scientific writing lacks the 'glamour' of other genres, but there's no reason why it should. Texts which inform and instruct, especially about difficult scientific concepts, could make exciting reading – like travel writing and science fiction, they can take us to new worlds. This section shows, therefore, how technical writing can have a powerful, creative impact on its readers. Key features: a desire to inform; precise references, often using specialist vocabulary; clear structure, an attempt to simplify the complicated . . .

Checking for Computer Viruses

from *Macintosh User's Guide (1991)*

Apple Computer Inc.

In recent years, 'viruses' – malicious programs that damage files or erase disks – have become a significant problem for people who use computers. A virus can be introduced into your Macintosh system from a disk you or someone else puts in a disk drive, from a network device such as a file server, or from an electronic bulletin board service.

You can use any of several virus-detection and -elimination programs to check your Macintosh disks for viruses. Such programs are available from user groups, computer bulletin boards, and dealers.

Even if you don't notice problems with your computer's operation or with the information on your disks, you should check for viruses frequently if you exchange disks or information with other users.

■ Whenever you get a disk from anyone – even if it's commercial software – check it for viruses before using it or copying anything from it to your hard disk.

■ Check your startup disk and other disks regularly with a virus-detection program and correct any problems it finds.

■ If your Macintosh is on a network or you use a modem to connect with information services or bulletin boards, check for viruses as often as it's practical – ideally, each time you copy any information from an outside source.

■ If you are part of a work group that includes a number of Macintosh users, set up a 'virus-detection station' that everyone can use to check disks (and to copy the latest version of the virus-detection software your group uses).

■ If you give information to other Macintosh users on disks or send information electronically, make certain that there are no viruses on your computer system before distributing the information.

■ Since new viruses appear regularly, make sure you have the latest version of any virus-detection software.

■ To avoid compatibility problems, be sure to use only one virus-detection program at a time.

Viruses – What They Are and How to Avoid Them

from *Murphy's Guide to DOS (Sybex Inc, 1993)*

by Sharon Crawford

Viruses are programs that are written with the deliberate intent of causing you and your computer grief. They range from the merely annoying to those that will destroy all the data on your hard disk.

If you only buy shrink-wrapped software from commercial outlets, never share disks with *anyone* else, never let anyone else use your computer, don't download programs from bulletin boards, and always wash your hands after using the bathroom, the chances of your getting a virus are very small. But if you work in an environment where computers are shared among several people, your chances of catching one of these bugs eventually is pretty high.

Where viruses come from

Viruses are written by computer vandals. Slimy little mole-like creatures whose blighted lives are devoted to making others as miserable as they are. They then take the product of their twisted psyches and put it on a bulletin board someplace, usually hidden inside a harmless-looking piece of shareware.

So a common source of computer viruses is a poorly supervised bulletin board. Since this is the province of nerds, you're unlikely to get one this way. But, if one of your friends or co-workers hands you a disk and tells you what a great new game he got, you might want to think twice about accepting the disk. In the first place, if the disk is commercial software, using it would be software piracy. Even more to the point, though, you have no idea where that disk has been. It could well harbour a virus, waiting to destroy your hard disk.

Murphy's Constant: Files will be damaged in direct proportion to their value.

Smile

from *Science 85*

by Alan Lightman

The woman's lips are glistening in the sunlight, reflecting high-density light on to the back of the man's retina.

It is an afternoon in March. A man and a woman stand on the wooden dock, gazing at the lake and the waves on the water. They haven't noticed each other.

The man turns. And so begins the sequence of biochemical events informing him of her. Light reflected from her body instantly enters the pupils of his eyes, at the rate of 10 trillion particles of light per second. Once through the pupil of each eye, the light travels through an oval-shaped lens, then through a transparent, jelly-like substance filling up the eyeball, and lands on the retina. Here it is gathered by a hundred million rod and cone cells.

Cells in the path of reflected highlights receive a great deal of light; cells falling in the shadows of the reflected scene receive very little. The woman's lips, for example, are just now glistening in the sunlight, reflecting light of high intensity on to a tiny patch of cells slightly north-east of back centre of the man's retina. The edges around her mouth, on the other hand, are rather dark, so that cells neighbouring the north-east patch receive much less light.

Each particle of light ends its journey to the eye upon meeting a retinene molecule, consisting of 20 carbon atoms, 28 hydrogen atoms, and one oxygen atom. In its doormat condition, each retinene molecule is attached to a protein molecule and has a twist between the 11th and 15th carbon atoms. But when light strikes it, as is now happening in about 30,000 trillion retinene molecules every second, the molecule straightens out and separates from its protein. After several intermediate steps, it wraps into a twist again, awaiting arrival of a new particle of light. Far less than a thousandth of a second has elapsed since this man saw that woman.

Triggered by the dance of the retinene molecules, the nerve cells, or neurons, respond. First in the eye and then in the brain. One neuron, for instance, has just gone into action. Protein molecules on its surface suddenly change their shape, blocking the flow of positively charged sodium atoms from the surrounding body fluid. This change in flow of electrically charged atoms produces a change in voltage that shudders through the cell. After a distance of a fraction of an inch, the electrical signal reaches the end of the neuron, altering the release of specific molecules, which migrate a distance of a hundred-thousandth of an inch until they reach the next neuron, passing along the news.

The woman, in fact, holds her hands by her sides and tilts her head at an angle of five and a half degrees. Her hair falls just to her shoulders. This information and much much more is exactingly encoded by the electrical pulses in the various neurons of the man's eyes.

In another few thousandths of a second, the electrical signals reach the ganglion neurons, which bunch together in the optic nerve at the back of the eye and carry their data to the brain. Here the impulses race to the primary visual cortex, a highly folded layer of tissue about a 10th of an inch thick and two square inches in area, containing 100 million neurons in half-a-dozen layers. The fourth layer receives the input first, does a preliminary analysis, and transfers the information to neurons in other layers. At every stage, each neuron may receive signals from a thousand other neurons, combine the signals – some of which cancel each other out – and dispatch the computed result to a thousand-odd other neurons.

After about 30 seconds – after several hundred trillion particles of reflected light have entered the man's eyes and been processed – the woman says hallo. Immediately, molecules of air are pushed together, then apart, then together, beginning in her vocal chords and travelling in a spring-like motion to the man's ears. The sound makes the trip from her to him (20 feet) in a 50th of a second.

Within each of his ears, the vibrating air quickly covers the distance to the eardrum. The eardrum, an oval membrane about 0.3 inch in diameter and tilted 55 degrees from the floor of the auditory canal, itself begins trembling and transmits its motion to three tiny bones. From there, the vibrations shake the fluid in the cochlea, which spirals snail-like two-and-a-half turns around.

Inside the cochlea the tones are deciphered. Here, a very thin membrane undulates in step with the sloshing fluid, and through this basilar membrane run tiny filaments of varying thicknesses, like strings on a harp. The woman's voice, from afar, is playing this harp. Her hallo begins in the low registers and rises in pitch toward the end. In precise response, the thick filaments in the basilar membrane vibrate first, followed by the thinner ones. Finally, tens of thousands of rod-shaped bodies perched on the basilar membrane convey their particular quiverings to the auditory nerve.

News of the woman's hallo, in electrical form, races along the neurons of the auditory nerve and enters the man's brain through the thalamus to a specialised region of the cerebral cortex for further processing.

Eventually, a large fraction of the trillion neurons in the man's brain become involved with computing the visual and auditory data just acquired. Sodium and potassium gates open and close. Electrical currents speed along neuron fibres. Molecules flow from one nerve ending to the next.

All of this is known. What is not known is why, after about a minute, the man walks over to the woman and smiles.

Study activities

Ghost stories

1 Think of any ghost stories you have heard – fictional or factual. In a small group, tell a couple of stories and then draw up a list of the essential ingredients in a written ghost story. Use these ideas as a starting-point, rejecting those you disagree with and adding more ideas of your own:

- believable central character
- powerful setting (e.g. old castle, abandoned school, etc.)
- plenty of description
- suspense
- happy ending.

2 How would a real-life ghost story differ from a made-up one? Try writing down the beginning of a supernatural experience someone has told you about, and see whether it feels different from a fictional tale. Is there any strong difference between fictional and non-fictional ghost stories, or do they all, finally, resemble fiction?

3 In *Not at Home*, what are the features which make it obviously a ghost story? Reread the opening of the story and decide at what point you can tell what the genre is. How can you tell: what in the story, style or language makes it *feel* like a ghost story?

4 One of the features of the story is that it doesn't use the usual creaky settings of many ghost stories. Write your own opening page of a ghost story set in an un-ghostly setting – for example, in a busy school, in a factory, at a swimmingpool. Pay close attention to building up a strong sense of place by giving plenty of precise details.

5 How do you explain the ending of Jean Rhys's story, *I Used to Live Here Once*?

6 The story is very brief – around 500 words – and yet we get a powerful visual sense of place. Look back at the story and consider how Jean Rhys makes the setting so vivid.

7 What do you think happens next? What does the girl do? Where does she go? What thoughts are running through her mind? Continue the story.

Crime fiction

1 Our society has an odd attitude towards crime: we seem obsessed with watching and reading about it, and yet also terrified. Make a list of all the crime shows you can think of on television, using two columns: 'Fictional' and 'Factual'. How many of them do you watch regularly? How do you explain our fascination with crime?

2 As drama work, take a fairy story like *Little Red Riding Hood* and present it in the style of a factual TV programme like *Crimewatch UK*. Work in a group of four (a, b, c and d), with each person taking on the different roles:

- a + b = TV presenters
- c = detective responsible for the case
- a = voice-over on reconstruction
- d = Little Red Riding Hood
- c = Grandma
- b = Wolf.

You might add other characters, such as eyewitnesses, to describe what they noticed. The important point when rehearsing your sketch is to treat the crime with complete seriousness – imitate the style of *Crimewatch UK* as closely as you can. Then present your sketch to the class. You could also write it up as a script.

3 Poet and thriller-reader T.S. Eliot wrote:

> In a detective story nothing should happen. The crime has already been committed, and the rest of the tale consists of the collection, selection and combination of evidence.

There are arguments for and against this. Such a story becomes a tale of detection – following the detective's attempts to untangle the mystery. But by the 1930s it had become a formula, and readers were shocked and excited when they read this:

> It was not until several weeks after he had decided to murder his wife that Dr Bickleigh took any active steps in the matter. Murder is a serious business. (Francis Iles, *Malice Aforethought*)

What is so radical here is that a murder is clearly waiting to happen. In small groups think of stories you have read and films or programmes you have seen which centre around crime. Try to think of examples of detective investigation as well as others in which a crime happens *during* the telling of the story. What is the appeal of the two different approaches?

In Ruth Rendell's story of *May and June*, look at the characters of the two sisters in the first four pages. What differences do you notice between them, and what similarities? Do these early pages contain any hints about what will happen at the end of the story?

4 Look at the comments of one student on the story:

> I thought it was spoilt by the characters' names – May, June and Avril. They made it seem unreal and difficult to believe. As a result I found that I didn't get involved in the story.

Do you agree? Is one essential ingredient of crime fiction that we have to feel deeply involved?

5 What do you imagine happens next? Does May's murder of her sister get found out by the police? How might they begin to suspect her? Continue the story. You could write it in the same third-person style (using *she* and *he*); or you may wish to change to a first-person narrative, writing now as if you are a detective inspector assigned to the case (using *I*).

Science fiction

1 Look at this comment by writer Theodore Sturgeon:

> A good science-fiction story is a story with a human problem, and a human solution, which would not have happened without its science content.

Think of some of the science-fiction stories you have read in books or seen on television or in the cinema. Do their story-lines deal with human problems caused by science? What part does the science content of the story play? Could the same story work just as well without any science content? Discuss your ideas.

2 Some people love science fiction. Other people hate it, finding it corny and ridiculous. Organise a debate in which a fan of science fiction defends it against someone who loathes it. Role-play the parts after you have made a list of the points that each side should make.

3 Look back at *The Forgotten Enemy*. How can we tell that the story is set in the future? What similarities does it have to the present? Are there any ways in which it feels like the past? Make a three-column list – past, present and future – and list some of the details from the story which fit into each column. For example, in the 'Past' column you could write – 'using coke for heating'.

4 Once Arthur C. Clarke has established Professor Millward's world, he begins to hint that something unexpected is happening. What clues can you find which show that this is no typical day?

5 What do you imagine happens next? The 'enemy he had forgotten' has returned. What can Professor Millward do? Should he even try to escape, or just accept the inevitable? Continue the story using the final paragraph as your starting-point. For a different twist on the tale, read Ted Hughes' poem 'October Dawn' about the onset of an ice age, and use it as the framework for your own story.

Horror

1 Some critics have suggested that horror stories and films are a way of coming to terms with our worst nightmares. What are your worst fears? Discuss your views in a small group.

2 Books like the 'Point Horror' series are very popular among young readers. Adult readers also buy many horror novels. But some people argue that they should not be read in schools because of their unpleasant themes and content. Organise a debate in which people argue for and against the presence of horror fiction in school libraries and

classrooms. You could then write up your ideas in a
discursive essay.

3 Some people seem to think that the horror genre only
appeals to men. Book sales and opinion polls show that this
is *not* the case: women as much as men read and write
horror stories. Undertake a survey in your class or year
group to find out who likes horror fiction. Find out why
they read it. Then write up your results in a factual
report.

4 Look back at the start of Ann Walsh's story, *Getting Away
from It All*. At what point could you tell that it was a horror
story? What were the exact clues? Near the end of the story
the narrative is interrupted, leaving the reader guessing:
what do you think happens at this point in the story?

5 Ann Walsh wrote about the origins of her tale:

In the early 1980s I became obsessed with purchasing a
summer retreat, a small cabin on a secluded lake where I
could 'get away from it all'. For a long two months one
summer, I dragged my children from one cottage to
another, never finding the place that I knew was the right
one. One day in August, a cloudy day with a hint of early
frost, we bumped our way over ten miles of bush road to a
deserted cabin on the shore of a lake that was as secluded
as anyone could desire.

That cabin had been deserted by humans, but not by the
rats. They had been everywhere; the furniture was
shredded, droppings crusted the floor and the air was thick
with their smell. My children announced that this place was
haunted and retreated rapidly to the car ... I never did tell
them that I, too, had caught the strangeness of that empty
cabin, had sensed the presence of ghosts that lived there
with the rats, waiting.

This story, 'Getting Away from It All', is how I laid those ghosts to rest, for what I had seen and sensed in that infested cabin haunted my dreams for many months.

This helps us to understand why authors write horror stories, but why do readers and cinema-goers read and watch them? Lisa Tuttle, who has edited a collection of horror stories, wrote:

Unlike a ride on the fairground ghost-train (or its cinematic equivalent), really effective horror fiction is a way of exploring areas of experience we normally access only in our dreams, if at all. (Introduction to *Skin of the Soul*, p. 1)

Does this feel right to you? Think of any stories from your own reading or viewing experience which have made a powerful impact on you, and think about why. Did they do more than simply shock you? Write a personal response to your own reading of the horror genre.

Travel writing

1 Critic and traveller Paul Fussell wrote: 'Before tourism there was travel, and before travel there was exploration . . . I am assuming that travel is now impossible and that tourism is all we have left . . . One who has hotel reservations and speaks no French is a tourist' (*Abroad*, p. 41). His point is that now it is almost impossible to explore places because everywhere has already been explored – except parts of the sea-bed and parts of the universe. As a result, Paul Fussell like many other writers is very hostile towards tourists.

What do you think? Is tourism so bad, or does it enable ordinary people (rather than just the wealthy) to see other

countries? Or has tourism made one place much like
another? Have a discussion about the difference between
travellers and tourists, using the points for and against in
this list:

For tourism	Against tourism
Allows more people to travel Makes travel cheaper Creates jobs Enables people to learn about the world	Destroys the environment People don't actually see the world – they just take their own culture with them Destroys local communities and traditions, or makes them into side-shows

2 Vivienne de Watteville arrived in Nairobi, Kenya, during the
1930s with dreams of going into 'the wilds unarmed' and
to 'win friendship with the beasts'. She also hoped to climb
Mount Kilimanjaro, the highest peak in Africa. In the extract
she is filming the wildlife. Pick out two sentences which show
her sense of wonder and excitement at what she observes.

3 British travellers in unfamiliar environments sometimes treat
the local people with little respect. What is Vivienne de
Watteville's attitude to the people she was with? Find some
examples to support your ideas.

4 Does the extract feel chiefly like a piece of travel writing or
an extract from an autobiography? What features make it
feel like either genre? Using two headings, make a list of
points in the text which could be used as evidence for
placing it in either genre.

5 Write about a place that you have explored – it can be near or far from home. Try to bring it vividly to life for the reader by describing it in detail.

6 What are Paul Theroux's main points about travel?

7 Paul Theroux begins by stating that 'there are two sorts of people who like trains'. What is your attitude towards train travel? When does it seem attractive and when does it seem irksome or tedious? Where would you like to travel by train? What advantages does train travel have over other forms? Discuss some of your ideas in a small group.

8 Theroux's article has a different feel to Vivienne de Watteville's. Where hers gave a chronological or narrative account of her experiences, Theroux is more concerned with the 'idea' of travel rather than a specific experience. Pick out a sentence from each which illustrates this different approach. Which text overall do you prefer?

9 Write your own article about a form of travel or a journey you have particularly enjoyed: it might even be your journey to school. As well as describing the journey itself, write about what you enjoy and dislike about this form of travel, and what you notice about fellow travellers. You might make it a humorous account.

Biography

1 Walk into any good bookshop and you will find a section filled with biographies. What is it that we like about reading about other people's lives? Look at these comments from different fans of biographies and discuss which you agree with and which you disagree with. Which, if any, comes closest to your own opinion?

a) Biographies allow me to escape from my own life into someone else's. They give me a chance to see through another person's eyes.

b) I think you find out about history much better in a biography than in a history book, because you see what people ate, drank, what they wore and what they worried about. Biography is history without all the theory.

c) They help you to understand human nature. Everyone is basically the same and biographies let us see what human beings are really like.

d) I like them because they encourage me to think what I would do if I was in that situation; so they're not simply about someone else's life – they force you to think about your own as well.

2 Look at the extract from the CD-ROM encyclopaedia. It gives us an outline of Roald Dahl's life. What do you like about the information? How clear is it – in its structure and its expression? Is anything lacking? What kind of information would you like to know that isn't contained here? What then is the purpose of a biographical encyclopaedia like this?

3 Write an encyclopaedia entry for your own life, or a parent or relative. Keep to the same format as the Encarta version, and limit yourself to just 150 words.

4 Jeremy Treglown's biography of Roald Dahl has been highly praised. Reviewers said it was:

'Fair-minded, funny and gently admonitory [critical]'
    Mail on Sunday
'calm, judicial, accurate, quietly brilliant' *Evening Standard*
'economical, lucid and convincing' *Independent on Sunday*
'excellent and briskly-paced' *Sunday Times*

Based on this brief extract, what is your impression of it?

5 Autobiography can sometimes feel like fiction – it uses characters, places, dialogue and tells a story. Pick out some sentences which give this biography a more factual feel – features that you would perhaps not expect in an autobiography.

6 Choose someone you know well – a relative or friend. Interview them, and write a two-page extract from their biography. Choose an event or experience which was particularly important to them. Then write a paragraph explaining how you decided to organise your account, what problems you encountered, and how well you think you have given the flavour of the person's life.

Autobiography

1 Why do you think people write their autobiographies – for money? So that their name lives on after their death? To explain why they behaved as they did? And why do people like to read them so much?

2 One problem with writing an autobiography is that the structure is fairly limited: you start at the beginning of your life and continue until the most recent point. Can you think of any ways of updating the genre? Would it be possible to write a 'backwards autobiography', or one which simply jumped backwards and forwards in time from one event to the next? Write an extract from your own autobiography, experimenting with an unexpected starting-point and unexpected shifts in time.

3 Read the extract from Roald Dahl's *Going Solo*. How does he make the story come to life? What techniques does he use to get and hold the reader's attention?

4 How does the event feel different from the way it was described in Jeremy Treglown's biographical account?

5 What do we learn about Roald Dahl's personality from this extract? Make a list of five words which describe him. For each one, find a quotation which supports your choice.

6 How would the 'Survival' extract differ if it was reduced to a 100-word summary written by a biographer for a collection of 'Important moments from writers' lives'? Will the story lose all of its drama and excitement? See if you can condense Roald Dahl's anecdote to the required length. Write in the third person mode (*he...* rather than *I...*).

Reportage

1 Reportage is an odd, French-sounding word, that you might not have heard of before. What does it mean? Writer and critic John Carey said this:

> Before editing a book of reportage you need to decide what reportage is, and how you tell the good from the bad. I decided early on that for my purposes reportage must be written by an eyewitness... Eyewitness accounts have the feel of truth because they are quick, subjective, and incomplete, unlike 'objective' or reconstituted history, which is laborious but dead. (Introduction to *The Faber Book of Reportage*, p. xxix)

Think of your own experience of eyewitness accounts – people talking on TV or radio after seeing an important event or disaster. What special quality does an eyewitness bring? What might be the disadvantages of this way of reporting events?

2 Television allows us to witness events 'live', which in the past newspaper readers would have waited to see reported at least a day later. Think of an event you have seen happening – either in front of you or through the media. Choose one that made an impact on you. In a small group, try to describe why it made such an impression.

3 Elizabeth Bentley's account of factory conditions is reported as an interview. Which of these words best describes the interviewer's tone of voice?

> shocked – angry – bitter – disbelieving – neutral – neutral at first, but increasingly involved – ashamed – emotional

Find evidence from the text to support your choice.

4 How would the account of the factory conditions be different if it was reported in paragraphs by the writer, rather than as an interview? Try converting the first part of it into a written account to see how it differs. Your first sentence might begin: 'I spoke to a millhand aged 23 who lived and worked in Leeds...'

5 Charles Dickens gave this account of life in the blacking warehouse to his biographer John Forster. You might feel that it resembles biography or autobiography more than reportage. It is included as reportage because of the immense visual detail Dickens uses, making it feel as if he is reliving the events of his childhood. Discuss the genre which you would use to classify the text – biography, autobiography, reportage.

6 Pick out a sentence that makes the memory of the warehouse seem very powerful. Then choose another that seems to resemble fiction – one of Dickens' stories – rather than real life.

7 How would you describe Dickens' attitude to what he describes? Choose one of the words from question 3 that feels most appropriate. Then find a quotation to support your choice.

8 Take the subject of the text and rewrite it or role-play it as an interview. The interviewer is finding out from Charles Dickens about life in the blacking warehouse. Try to make the physical conditions of the place come alive as powerfully as possible.

Diaries

1 Actor Kenneth Williams kept a diary all his life. On Tuesday 8 March 1988 he ponders why people keep diaries:

> The preoccupation with diary writing is caused by various things: the desire to keep a record which can be useful later, and committing to paper what can't be communicated to a mentor . . . oh! All kinds of reasons, but *fundamentally* it is about loneliness. (*The Kenneth Williams Diaries*, ed. Russell Davies, 1993)

How much truth do you think there is in this? What other reasons might there be for people to keep diaries?

2 Do you keep a diary, or have you done so in the past? What was your purpose? Who were you writing to – just yourself? Who would you allow to see what you had written? On what occasions did you find you wrote the most?

3 Many diaries are filled with accounts of trivial events. Cynthia Asquith's diary entry deals with a dreadful personal loss – the death of her brother at war. How does she use her diary to express her emotion? Can you find evidence that the writing process helps her to come to terms with the event?

4 Edward R. Murrow's diary records the beginning of the Blitz – the period in 1940 when London and other cities were regularly bombed by German planes. The extract finishes, 'This night bombing is serious and sensational.' How would you describe Murrow's overall attitude to what he experiences?

5 The extract contains a number of terms which you might not be sure about – such as V-formation, shrapnel, air-raid shelters, anti-aircraft fire. Scan the text for any other examples and then see whether other people in your class can clarify the meanings of any of the terms.

6 How does the extract differ in its language from a newspaper report or war story? Write the first paragraph of a newspaper report on the start of the Blitz, based on the information in the extract; then write the first few paragraphs of a fictional account of the same material. How did your use of language differ? Write a paragraph analysis of what you have written, explaining the decisions you made and how well the two pieces work.

Letters

1 You might think that modern technology would make letter-writing a thing of the past. Yet fax machines and e-mail have encouraged people to keep writing letters while allowing them to be delivered up to thousands of miles away within seconds. What are some of the advantages of written communication over spoken? When does a letter seem better suited to our purpose than a telephone conversation?

Look at this jumbled list of points and decide whether they belong to written or spoken communication. Some might belong to both columns, or you might simply be unsure.

Written communication?	Spoken communication?
a) you can make sure that the person you are addressing understands you b) you can go back over the message several times c) it is permanent d) it is better suited to formal situations	e) it is quicker to express your ideas f) it is less emotional g) almost everyone can use it – it doesn't need to be learned h) it is better for saying something sensitive i) it is more pleasant to receive

2 Charlotte Brontë – author of the Victorian novel *Jane Eyre* – writes to her publisher about the death of her brother, Branwell. What features does this have of written rather than spoken English – in its layout, language and structure? What is Charlotte Brontë able to do in writing which would have been more difficult in speech?

3 Wilfred Owen writes to his mother from the trenches of northern France in World War I. It is partly about what has happened to him, and partly about the state of his own frayed emotions. Which sentence is the most factual? Which is the most emotional?

4 How do you imagine Wilfred Owen's mother would react to the letter? Was he right to send it, or should he have spared her feelings? Discuss this in a small group.

5 Writing from a different standpoint and for a different purpose, Bertrand Russell writes about the same war as

Wilfred Owen. His letter, addressed to the editor of the newspaper the *Nation*, is public rather than personal. It doesn't, for example, have an element of story-telling in it: instead it is concerned with ideas. Pick out three examples of the style and language which show that this is a public rather than private letter.

6 Although you will be able to follow the gist of Bertrand Russell's letter, he uses some very precise, obscure vocabulary. Try rewriting his text as a 50-word letter to a modern tabloid newspaper – one where we expect the vocabulary to be simpler and the message more direct. What do you lose and gain in the process?

7 Tracey Cramton's letter is different again in style and purpose. It reminds us of the vast variety of letters there can be. In it she is writing for advice from the 'problem page' of *Practical Fishkeeping* magazine. Do you find the letter and its reply factual, sad, funny, surprising? Discuss your response and try to explain it.

8 Why do people often prefer to write for advice rather than speak to someone directly? (Think about newspaper and magazine problem pages.) What advantage does written communication give both the reader and the writer?

Speeches

1 Some people believe that the art of speech-making is dying out. Who needs to address a crowd of a thousand in a hall or conference centre, when you can talk through the airwaves to five million people in their own sitting-rooms? Think of speeches you hear in person – assemblies, prize-

days, some lessons perhaps ... Do you think that speeches
will be necessary in the future or will technology make
them redundant?

2 Think of the public speakers you have heard – for example,
the different speakers who address you in assemblies. Which
speakers make the strongest impact upon you? Why? What
special skills do they have? In pairs or a small group, draw up
a list of ingredients for the elements of a good speech or
assembly – both for its content and its performance.

3 Chief Seattle's speech is an unusual one. It was spoken to a
transcriber, who wrote it out and then delivered the written
version to the President of the USA in 1854. In it, he gives
up territory of the native Indians to the American State –
and is deeply uneasy in doing so. Read the speech aloud if
you can. How does Chief Seattle use language to make his
message persuasive? (Look at the use of repetition and the
use of emotive, often abstract words, such as *man, family,
beasts, Creator.*)

4 What is the basic message of Chief Seattle's speech?

5 Emmeline Pankhurst was a powerful and effective
campaigner for the rights of women. With the outbreak of
World War I she encouraged women to join the armed
forces or go into industry, to help with the war effort. In
July 1915 thirty thousand women marched through
London with the slogan, 'We demand the right to serve.'
What are the main points she makes in her speech? Which
parts do you find most persuasive? How does she use
humour to support her case?

6 Mrs Pankhurst's speech feels very different from Chief
Seattle's – obviously in its content, but also in style and
tone. What differences do you notice?

7 Take an issue you feel strongly about – treatment of animals, whaling, Third World exploitation – and write your own speech persuading people to your own viewpoint. Remind yourself of some of the techniques used in the speeches in this book, and experiment with them in your own written speech.

Technical writing

1 The term 'technical writing' is used here to describe texts which are chiefly concerned with giving information – textbooks, manuals, leaflets, instructions, guides and so on. Make a list of the different pieces of instructional writing you have read in the past twenty-four hours (remember to include texts such as road signs).

2 Recipe books are one popular form of technical writing. Do a survey of different forms of recipes and the way the information is structured and presented. Some books have introductions about the region where the recipe or ingredients are found. Some use bullet points to give quick instructions. Some use technical language. Some use illustrations to clarify each step. Compare a supermarket recipe card with two or three different recipe books, and describe the differences you notice in their language and presentation. Write your survey up as a report.

3 The first text about computer viruses is taken from a computer manual. How can you tell? What clues are there in the vocabulary and the way the writing is structured?

4 On a scale of 1 (low) to 10 (high), how clear to follow is the text? What would you do to make it clearer to understand?

5 The second extract about computer viruses is from a handbook called *Murphy's Guide to DOS*. It is a book aimed at explaining technical details about computers to readers who don't see themselves as technical. What do you notice are the main differences from the computer manual text – in layout and language?

6 The writer uses quite a lot of informal words and phrases, like those listed below. For each one, write down a more formal way of saying the same thing:

- pretty high
- causing grief
- you're unlikely to get one this way.

Now find some terms which you think may be too technical or complex for general readers, and see if you can think of a more informal way of saying the same thing.

7 Alan Lightman takes one of the everyday processes we take for granted, and shows us scientifically what is happening. What are the main events which, according to him, are taking place when one person responds to another? Try to summarise his text into 3 to 6 points.

8 When you started to read the extract you could be forgiven for thinking that it was the opening of a story. Look at the opening sentences. What makes them feel different from our expectations of technical writing? Where precisely does the style of writing change?

9 Choose a process you know something about – changing a bicycle tyre or installing some computer software – and write your own instructions, aimed at a general reader. You might use some of the techniques seen in the extracts here, for example subheadings and bullet points.

Selected authors

Lady Cynthia Asquith (1887–1960) was born into the upper classes and married the son of a Prime Minister in 1910. Her diaries, however, remain intensely personal and show her deeply mixed feelings about World War I.

Charlotte Brontë (1816–55) lived with her family in the bleak isolated village of Haworth, Yorkshire, where she wrote her famous novel *Jane Eyre*. Her brother Branwell tried to make his name as a poet and painter, but sank into a life of drink and despair.

Roald Dahl (1916–90) was born in Wales of Norwegian parents. He is undoubtedly one of the world's most popular authors, adored by children and read with misgivings by some adults because of the nature of his stories' subject matter.

John Forster (1812–76) was a journalist and biographer, and a friend of Charles Dickens. Upon Dickens' death he wrote the first biography of the great writer.

Edward R. Murrow (1908–65) was a famous American broadcaster who came to London in 1937. His descriptive broadcasts to America brought home the reality of World War II to an American audience.

Wilfred Owen (1893–1918) was born in Shropshire and, at the age of twenty-two, enlisted in the army. His poetry and letters show how deeply the horrors of trench warfare – the gas, the cold, the ugliness – affected him. On 4 November 1918, one week before the end of World War I, he was killed leading his men across the Sambre Canal in France.

Emmeline Pankhurst (1858–1928) founded the Women's Social and Political Union to fight for the rights of women. After the bombing by the WSPU of Prime Minister Lloyd George's home in 1913, she was arrested and imprisoned thirteen times under the notorious 'Cat and Mouse Act'. This allowed prisoners on hunger-strike to be released and then, once their health was regained, they would be rearrested.

Jean Rhys (*c*. 1890–1919) was born in Dominica in the West Indies. She is best known as the author of *Wide Sargasso Sea*, a retelling of Charlotte Brontë's *Jane Eyre* from Bertha Mason's (Mrs Rochester's) point of view.

Bertrand Russell (1872–1970) is probably the most famous philosopher of the twentieth century. His early writing was concerned with mathematics, but he extended his thinking to questions about our senses and the external world. He was politically active, with a hatred of war, and fought for the rights of conscientious objectors – people unwilling to fight in war because of their moral objections.

Chief Seattle (*c*. 1784–1866) was Chief of the North American Dwamish, Suquamish and allied Indian tribes, who negotiated on their behalf with the US Government. In 1855 he signed the Treaty of Point Elliot giving up lands in Washington State. He was anxious that the settlement should not be named after him because he believed that after death his spirit would be disturbed every time his name was spoken.

Vivienne de Watteville (1900–57) had a passion for travelling. Although she never achieved her ambition of climbing Mount Kilimanjaro, she did live for a time in a hut on neighbouring Mount Kenya.

Further reading

Fiction genres

The following books all make good introductions to their different genres:

Ghost stories: Robert Westall (ed.), *Ghost Stories* (Kingfisher, 1989)

Crime fiction: Maxim Jakubowski (ed.), *Murders for the Fireside* (Pan, 1992)

Science fiction: Brian Aldiss (ed.), *The Penguin Science Fiction Omnibus* (Penguin, 1973)

Horror: Lisa Tuttle (ed.), *Skin of the Soul: New Horror Stories by Women* (The Women's Press, 1990)

Non-fiction genres

Travel writing: Eric Newby (ed.), *A Book of Travellers' Tales* (Picador, 1986)

Travel writing: Linda Marsh (ed.), *Travel Writing* (Longman Imprint Books, 1996)

Biography and autobiography: Kenneth and Valerie McLeish, *The Bloomsbury Good Reading Guide to Biography and Autobiography* (Bloomsbury, 1992)

Autobiography: Linda Marsh (ed.), *Autobiographies* (Longman Imprint Books, 1992)

Reportage: John Carey (ed.), *The Faber Book of Reportage* (Faber, 1989)

Diaries and letters: Celeste Flower (ed.), *Diaries and Letters* (Longman Imprint Books, 1996)

Diaries: Ronald Blythe (ed.), *The Penguin Book of Diaries* (Penguin, 1991)

Letters: Felix Pryor (ed.), *The Faber Book of Letters* (Faber, 1988)

Speeches: Brian MacArthur (ed.), *The Penguin Book of Twentieth-Century Speeches* (Penguin, 1993)

Technical Writing: Bernard Dixon (ed.), *From Creation to Chaos: Classic Writings in Science* (Abacus, 1993)

Further reading projects

1 Choose a genre you have found particularly interesting and compile your own collection of five to eight recommended texts. Then write an introduction which introduces the texts to a general reader.

2 Write a review of one of the texts featured here. Say what you like about the way it has been structured and what you dislike. What are the highlights? How could the text be improved?

Acknowledgements

We are grateful to the following for permission to reproduce copyright material.

the author's agent for the short story 'The Forgotten Enemy' from *Of Time and Stars* by Arthur C Clarke (Victor Gollancz); the author's agent for an extract from *Going Solo* by Roald Dahl (Jonathan Cape Ltd and Penguin Books Ltd); EMAP Pursuit Publishing Ltd for an extract from *Practical Fishkeeping* October 1993; Faber & Faber Ltd for an extract from *Roald Dahl* by Jeremy Treglown; Hodder Headline Plc for the short story 'Not at Home' by Jean Richardson from *Cold Feet* ed. Jean Richardson (Hodder & Stoughton, 1989); Pavilion Books for the extract 'This is London' by Edward R Murrow from *How It Was in the War* edited by Godfrey Smith; Penguin Books Ltd for the short story 'I Used to Live Here Once' from *Sleep it off Lady* by Jean Rhys (Penguin Books 1979, first published by Andre Deutsch, 1976) copyright © Jean Rhys, 1976 and extracts from the short story 'Stranger on a Train: The Pleasures of Railways' from *Sunrise with Seamonsters* by Paul Theroux (Hamish Hamilton, 1985) copyright © Cape Cod Scriveners Co, 1985; Random House UK Ltd on behalf of the Estate of Cynthia Asquith for an extract from *Lady Cynthia Asquith: Diaries 1915–1918* (Hutchinson); Reed Consumer Books Ltd for an extract from *Speak to the Earth: Wanderings and Reflections Among Elephants and Mountains* by Vivienne de Watteville (Methuen); the author's agent for the short story 'May and June' from *Collected Short Stories* by Ruth Rendell (Hutchinson); The Bertrand Russell Peace Foundation Ltd for Bertrand Russell's letter to the *Nation* newspaper 15 August 1914 © The Bertrand Russell Peace Foundation Ltd; the author, Ann Walsh for her short story 'Getting Away From it All' and an extract from the Afterword from *Skin of the Soul* ed. Lisa Tuttle (The Woman's Press, 1990).

We have unfortunately been unable to trace the copyright holder of 'Smile' by Alan Lightman in *From Creation to Chaos* ed. Bernard Dixon and would appreciate any information which would enable us to do so.

Cover by Ship

Pearson Education Limited
Edinburgh Gate, Harlow,
Essex, CM20 2JE, England.

This educational edition first published 1996
Fourth impression 1999

Editorial material set in 10/12.5 pt Stone Sans
Printed in Singapore (PH)

ISBN 0 582 25391 8

The publisher's policy is to use paper manufactured from
sustainable forests.